A SMALL BOOK OF PRAYERS FOR GREAT BIG POWER

ERICA DIGGS

CONTENTS

DEDICATION

I dedicate my first book to my husband, mom, pastor, friends, and all Christians everywhere who want more of the power of God in their everyday lives.

To my husband:

Thank you, honey, for continually believing in me and encouraging me to write this book. I love how you inspire me to be better by your example. Your get-it-done-now attitude has helped me and motivated me to complete this project. You have written several books. When I saw what you accomplished, I knew I could do the same. You are a blessing, and you lovingly show me every day that you are my greatest supporter. I am truly thankful for you.

To my mom:

Mother, you are full of love and kindness. I grew up listening to your prayers. You were the first one to teach me how to pray. You were and still are diligent and disciplined to pray for your family every day without ceasing. You have taught me to be fervent in prayer and to never give up, no matter how long it takes. Your prayers for the lost and your treatment of those who have mistreated you have shown me Jesus's way of loving people on earth. I am truly grateful for your example of prayer.

To my pastor:

A special thanks goes to my spiritual father, Pastor Robert Scales. Thank you for your labor in the Word and in prayer so that you could feed your flock so well. You have continually birthed the message of love and faith in me for years. I am always blessed by our services, and I leave church knowing I can conquer the world through Jesus. The greatest message you ever taught me was to know what Jesus taught, said, and did for us in the Word and on the cross. I now know what it truly means to love others the way Jesus loves me. You have never wavered from Jesus's teachings, and because of what you have taught me, I now walk in victory in my everyday life.

To my friends:

Friends, your love, support, and prayers have inspired me to write. Your constant questions and enthusiasm about the things of God encourage me daily. You have interceded for me and co-labored with me on many prayer assignments. Together, we have seen the Lord do many miraculous things in response to prayer. We are truly better together. I love you all so much.

I want to send a special thank you to my friends who helped me specifically with this book. I persevered to the finish line because you all prayed, offered advice, read for me, listened, and encouraged me through this whole process. I am eternally grateful for your love and friendship.

I dedicate this book to all the Christians who have been in hard battles and who feel as if they are losing. I also dedicate this book to Christians who are hungry for more of God's glory and who are determined to walk in the power that we have been given by Jesus. Jesus said in Luke 10:19, "Behold, I give unto you power and authority over all the power that the enemy possesses, and nothing shall by any means hurt you."

I was inspired to write this book of prayers because of the many encounters that I have experienced ministering to people in various places. I have shared with people in jails, rescue missions, hospitals, nursing homes, on the phone, in pulpits, home Bible studies, schools, camps, and more. People always asked me if I could send them a text or a copy of what I just said or prayed. Then they would ask for a copy of my notes. At a mom's Bible study, one mom asked me if I had ever thought about writing a book with the prayers that I pray daily. When we left that night, my husband stated that I needed to write the book as soon as possible. That was when I first knew God had called me to write this book.

This book gives you a bit of insight into my personal prayer life, relationship with God, and fellowship with my Lord and Savior Jesus Christ. In *A Small Book of Prayers*, you will see just a bit of what has made me a successful Christian throughout the years.

This book has been influenced by great faith teachers, including Pastor Robert Scales, Kenneth E. Hagin, Billye Brim, Oral Roberts, Norvel Hayes, Keith Moore, Kenneth and Gloria Copeland, Andrew Wommack, Fred Price, Bill Winston, Charles Capps, and others.

LETTER FROM THE EDITOR

Dear Reader,

I work as a full-time editor and have edited nearly 150 books in the last eleven years or so. Nearly all my business comes from past clients, referrals, or social media interactions. But Erica didn't connect with me in any of the usual ways.

The story of how I came to edit *A Small Book of Prayers for Great Big Power* is truly a divine connection. Erica's husband, LaJuan, searched online for a Christian editor. He looked over my website and then contacted me on Facebook. After briefly chatting with him over Messenger, I called Erica. After further discussion, she and LaJuan agreed that I was right for this project. And I'm so glad they chose me.

When I first read the sample Erica sent, I was thrilled. This book is filled with powerful prayers to encourage the reader. Every prayer is packed with Scripture. In fact, I can honestly say that for its length, this book has more Bible verses than almost any book I've ever edited.

At one point, I was reviewing a section of the book with Erica. I stopped and exclaimed, "My faith is being built up right now by the Word as I am editing!" We both laughed as we were encouraged by the Lord.

I was so honored to work on this book. My prayer for you, the reader, is that your faith will be strengthened as well as you pray these prayers and allow the Lord to minister to you.

God bless you,
Lisa Thompson
<u>www.writebylisa.com</u>

INTRODUCTION

I pray that this book of prayers will change your life forever and encourage you in your growth to greater spiritual maturity. It is my hope and prayer that you will use this book and refer to it often as a means of overcoming life's daily struggles and the forces of darkness.

I was inspired to write this book because I have seen many people struggle to get answers to simple and complex prayers. They would often become angry, blame God, and wonder why they did not receive what they had hoped to receive in prayer. This book seeks to explain biblical truths concerning prayer, show what faith truly is, and give practical examples of prayer based on the Word of God. The explanations and examples given are meant to help answer the question of how to pray effectively to see results. The same power that Jesus walked in while He was on the earth is available to us because He said that He gave it to us in Luke 10:19. Jesus laid hands on the sick and they recovered, He opened blind eyes, healed the lepers, cleansed people of their sins, healed the brokenhearted, changed spiritual conditions, raised the dead, and more.

Jesus told us in John 14:12 that, "He that believeth on me, the works that I do shall he do also; and greater works than these shall he do; because I go unto my Father." This should be the expectation of anyone who says that they are a child of the living God. For God is a Creator and a miracle worker, and He still wants to perform miracles for us today because He loves us. The only condition to performing miracles as Jesus did is putting faith in how much Jesus loves us and what that love has done for us, which causes us to believe on Him and His promises. This is not just simply saying that we believe; we must learn how to trust in, cling to, and rely on Jesus in spite of what our physical senses may be telling us about our current conditions. To do this, we must become seasoned in the Word of God. If we can allow the mind of Christ to become our mindset, we will be ready to apply and do what Jesus taught us and see His results. He taught in Mark 16:17–18 that "these signs shall follow them that believe; in my name shall they cast out devils; they shall speak with new tongues; they shall take up serpents; and if they drink any deadly thing, it shall not hurt them; they shall lay hands on the sick, and they shall recover."

As a sickly child growing up, this passage of Scripture fascinated me, and I often wondered if it was really true. I sought the Lord to teach me about healing, faith, and how to believe in this manner. I wanted to see the signs and wonders for myself that Jesus promised would be given to those who believed on Him. I was desperate for healing after many years of battling with asthma, allergies, sinus issues, and bronchitis. I was born six weeks early, and my lungs were underdeveloped as a baby. Therefore, I was never allowed to go outside and play as my siblings, family, and the other children in the neighborhood did. For I struggled most of my childhood just to breathe, and as a result, I was dependent upon many medications and missed many days from school. In fact, a teacher had to come to my home my junior year of high school so that I could stay on track with my studies.

I prayed to God one day and said, "If You are really real, then I want You to heal me so that I will not need to take any medications for the rest of my life." As I studied the Word of God and learned about where sicknesses and diseases came from and how Jesus defeated every sickness and every disease on the cross, I gained confidence in God and in His Word. I began to rise up and fight spiritually for my healing through prayer. God showed me the power that He had given me as a believer by answering my prayer and many, many more. Today, I am not on any medications, and I only take a vitamin if I want to.

Not only did the Lord heal my physical condition, but He healed me spiritually and emotionally from growing up in a broken home. Unfortunately, I grew up in a household filled with domestic violence. My dad physically and verbally abused my mother. My parents were divorced when I was ten, and from that moment on, my mother struggled financially to provide for me and my siblings. As a result, she suffered from depression, which caused a ripple effect in our home. Further, I had a friend who committed suicide when I was in high school. This left us even more depressed, broke, busted, and disgusted with life. However, no matter how difficult things seemed, my mother never quit praying for us. We could hear her praying early in the morning hours, crying out to God to save her and her family. I will never forget those prayers as long as I live.

So the depression continued, and after losing some of these difficult battles with depression and anger, I knew that I was in serious need of a Savior. I wanted out of the cycles of misery and pain. What joy I found when I learned that Jesus was my hope and the answer for a better life and future. Today, I am thankful to say that as a wife and mother of three strong kings, I used the power of prayer to fight my past and keep it from negatively affecting my future and the future of those I love the most. Please understand that how we live can severely impact those around us in a negative or positive way.

God also gave me a great pastor who taught me the importance of knowing Jesus's words and reminding God of His Word and promises in prayer. After many years of studying the Scriptures, God then sent me into the prisons, nursing homes, hospitals, missions, schools, other churches, and more to be the hands and feet of Christ. When we operate as His body, we will preach the gospel, lay hands on the sick, watch them recover, cast out devils, operate in authority, heal the brokenhearted, be a peacemaker, set the captives free, and get others filled with the Spirit. Being a true born-again child of God, who is love, will motivate you to want to be and live just like love. You will want to give others the compassion of the Lord like He freely gave us and see them be completely set free from the cruelties of this world.

With this hope in mind, the Lord has sent me on many assignments to teach His people the basics of faith and the promises of God for their particular circumstances. Once they learned their rights as God's children, they could use His power to put Satan and his demons on the run and walk in victory. Now I have great joy in seeing people healed from life-threatening illnesses, depression, worry, stress, poverty, hatred, strife, anxiety, unforgiveness, sin, doubt, unbelief, and more. I even saw my oldest son's knee completely and supernaturally healed after it was blown out during a football game.

He was told he may never play sports again and that it would take eight months to a year before he could try and play after surgery. My son opted not to have the surgery. Instead, we found healing verses in the Bible and took the Word like medicine three times a day. We used the power of agreement with other fellow believers, quoted the Word, prayed the Word, reminded God of His promises, worshipped the Lord as our miracle-working God, and watched God perform a supernatural miracle in six weeks. Yes, he was back on the field playing football in six weeks!

The power of prayer is real. I pause here to give God all the glory, honor, and praise for loving us and showing us His power in this manner. We know during times like these, we need all of the encouragement we can get. Don't ever underestimate the power of prayer, worship, the Word of God, and watching videos of testimonies of God's powerful intervention in someone else's life. These actions help to build trust and confidence that God can and will do the same thing for you. Glory to God for the Word, which is the substance for a strong prayer life when praying to the Father.

We know that the entire Bible from Genesis to Revelation is the divinely inspired Word of God by the Holy Spirit. It is God's counsel, plans, and purposes through different ages and dispensations for three groups of people: the Jews, the nations, and the church. For this reason, we should seek God's Word for answers to problems and remind Him of His promises on a daily basis. This book uses many Scriptures from the Old and New Testament that a believer in Christ can stand on, believe, and speak in prayer to experience triumph and see miracles occur.

The Holy Spirit helps us know how God's Word should be applied in every situation. For example, when we read 2 Timothy 3:16–17 in the Amplified Bible, Classic Edition, we can see how God uses the Holy Spirit and his Word to transform us into the image of Christ. This passage says that "Every scripture is God-breathed, (given by His inspiration) and profitable for instruction, for reproof, and conviction of sin, for correction of error and discipline in obedience, [and] for training in righteousness (holy living, in conformity to God's will in thought, purpose, and action, So that the man of God may be complete and proficient, well fitted and thoroughly equipped for every good work." We need the whole counsel of God from Genesis to Revelation to be ready for *every* good work. So, inspiration, cleansing, and washing happens to us when we read the Scriptures and pray them back to the Father. We should want the Lord to fine-tune or correct, heal, and empower us through prayer. Praying the Word of God daily will naturally cause this to happen.

When we allow God's presence to transform us in prayer, we become and operate just like Him on the earth. This is why Jesus came to the earth. He wanted to show us the Father's love and power, defeat sin in the flesh, make one new man, and to make disciples. A disciple is a learner. Jesus told His disciples to go into the world and preach the gospel to every creature. He told them to go and make disciples. (See Matthew 28:19 and Mark 16:15.) Imagine someone learning from Jesus how to pray to the Father. This is precisely what happened in Luke 11:1. "As he was praying in a certain place, when he ceased, one of his disciples said to him, Lord, teach us to pray, as John also taught his disciples" (KJV). Jesus then went on to teach His learners about God's character, how to approach God, and what to say in prayer. Today, the Holy Spirit leads and guides us in prayer, but we can still be Jesus's disciple by following His teachings.

For years, my pastor has often preached and even told me personally that "a disciple takes the teachings of their master and makes them their rule of conduct." Therefore, we need to hear what Jesus taught, said, and did and make His teachings our rule of conduct or the way we live every day. The body of

Christ needs His teachings as the foundation to our faith. Jesus said in Luke 6:47–49 that the person who comes to Him hears what He says and does it. That person has built his house upon the rock, and the gates of hell cannot prevail against that person or his foundation. This Scripture shows the importance of Jesus's words and why they are the building blocks and basis of what we believe and speak daily. We should make sure that we are using His words when praying to the Father.

When I talk about the teachings of Christ, I am not just talking about the Gospels. However, I do believe His teachings in the Gospels should be supreme. My pastor has shown me the importance of elevating Christ's teachings in our thinking and making them the primary focus in our everyday lives. In saying that, I firmly believe that the Scriptures should not be divided in an either/or manner. For the whole Bible is God's counsel and plan to three different groups of people and should be viewed as His instructions to each. Oh, how I love the whole counsel of God from Genesis to Revelations!

We learn so much about God and prayer from the prophets, but we want to make sure that we are following Jesus in our everyday lives. John 1:17 in the The Passion Translation also makes a distinction by saying, "Moses gave us the Law, but Jesus, the Anointed One, unveils truth wrapped in tender mercy." Therefore, if we want "the truth" that makes us free from *all* the power the enemy possesses, then we have to continue in Jesus's words, hold fast to His teachings, and live in accordance with them. Doing this makes us His true followers and releases true freedom in our lives in every area. We can see this in John 8:31-32 in the Amplified Bible Classic Edition.

Further, this next passage of scripture shows us why what Jesus taught, said, and did for us is so important. Second John 1:9–11 says,

> Anyone who runs on ahead [of God] and does not abide in the doctrine of Christ [who is not content with what He taught] does not have God; but he who continues to live in the doctrine (teaching) of Christ [does have God], he has both the Father and the Son. If anyone comes to you and does not bring this doctrine [is disloyal to what Jesus Christ taught], do not receive him [do not accept him, do not welcome or admit him] into [your] house or bid him Godspeed or give him any encouragement. For he who wishes him success [who encourages him, wishing him Godspeed] is a partaker in his evil doings. (AMPC)

In these verses, we can see that if we do not have Christ's teachings, then we do not have God working. Further, in John 6:28, the disciples asked Jesus, "What shall we do, that we might work the works of God? Jesus answered and said unto them, "This is the work of God, that ye believe on *him* whom he hath sent" (KJV). Notice, while answering this question Jesus did not send them to works, their own strength, or ability as a means of justifying God's works. Instead, He instructed them to believing on Him, which causes God to work in every area as you apply His teachings. This is how you get answers to prayer. For, God performs and responds to His word.

We must realize that the Father sent Jesus in His name to represent Him exactly and act on His behalf. Colossians 1:15 states that Jesus "is the exact likeness of the unseen God [the visible representation of the invisible]; He is the Firstborn of all creation" (AMPC). We see in Colossians 2:15 that Jesus also defeated and disarmed the devil and his demons. He taught in John 14:6 that He was the way, the truth, and the life. He said no one could come to the Father but by Him. This is even in prayer. We need to come to the Father in Jesus's name when praying. In the same token, when Peter wanted to build a tabernacle for Jesus, Moses, and Elijah in Luke 9:35, the Father's voice came through the clouds and said, "This is my Son, my Chosen One. Listen to Him" (NLT). The Father never pointed us to anyone else but the Son. Philippians 2:5 instructs us to "Let this mind be in you, which was also in Christ Jesus." You get his mindset by meditating on His teachings in the Word of God and observing to do them.

The book of Ephesians tells us that Jesus is now seated at the right hand of the Father in heaven. This means that Jesus has equal power, authority, honor, position, success, strength, intelligence, might, victory, and dignity as our almighty God. Because of Jesus's special seat or place on the throne beside the Father, God has highly exalted Him above all the works of darkness. Therefore, if we take our seat of authority with Jesus and reign in this life as a king with Him, we will be far above all principalities, powers, might, dominion, and every name that is named on this earth. For God put everything under Jesus's feet and made Him to be the head over all things to the church.

Truly, it is very important to understand your position of authority beside Jesus. Not only do we need to understand it, but we must know how to use it to pray effectively and get results. God also gave Jesus the name that is above every name. That at the name of Jesus, demons tremble and must flee. However, just because Jesus is seated with the Father in heaven does not mean that Jesus has left us alone in the earth.

When Jesus left the earth to be with the Father, God sent us the wonderful Holy Spirit to take His place. The Holy Spirit came to represent Jesus and act on His behalf, helping God's children. The Holy Spirit also has the responsibility of revealing Christ in us as believers and making clear to us what God has already done. We need a revelation or understanding of what it means to have Christ in us as the hope of glory. This means that when we have Jesus living in our hearts, God's manifested presence or glory can be upon us and operate through us. But without the person of the Holy Spirit, we would not be able to understand the things of God. Let's look more closely at the role of the Holy Spirit.

The Holy Spirit's job can be clearly seen in John 14:26, which says, "But the Comforter (Counselor, Helper, Intercessor, Advocate, Strengthener, Standby), the Holy Spirit, Whom the Father will send in My name [in My place, to represent Me and act on My behalf], He will teach you all things. And He will cause you to recall (will remind you of, bring to your remembrance) everything I have told you" (AMPC). When we listen to the Holy Spirit, He will lead and guide us into *all* truth. The good news is that God's Word in Luke 11:13 says that God gives the Holy Spirit to those who ask Him. He is a free gift!

Further, the Holy Spirit teaches us how to pray. Romans 8:26 says that He comes to our aid and bears us up in our weaknesses (AMPC). He does this because we do not know what prayer to offer or how to offer it worthily as we ought. Therefore, the Holy Spirit makes intercession or prays for us. He will pray through us if we yield to Him. Because of His role in the lives of believers, we begin to see and operate in more and more of the power of God. Thank God for the Holy Spirit. When the Holy Spirit teaches us how to pray, we will be unstoppable in prayer. He will show us how to get every prayer answered, every time, in every way, in Jesus's name.

Prayer is communication, relationship, and fellowship with our almighty God and not a show or a contest. Jesus taught us in Matthew 6:5–8,

> And when thou prayest, thou shalt not be as the hypocrites are: for they love to pray standing in the synagogues and in the corners of the streets, that they may be seen of men. Verily I say unto you, they have their reward. But thou, when thou prayest, enter into thy closet, and when thou hast shut thy door; pray to thy Father which is in secret; and thy Father which seeth in secret shall reward thee openly. But when ye pray, use not vain repetitions, as the heathen do: for they think that they shall be heard of their much speaking. Be not ye therefore like unto them: for your Father knoweth what things ye have need of, before ye ask him. (KJV)

Lots of lessons can be learned from these verses. Firstly, we should make sure that we approach God with the proper motivation. We must not have a wrong attitude or agenda. The proper motivation behind our prayers should be to experience the Father's love and not just to complain or express a want or a need. Praying about our needs has its place, but that should not be our sole purpose. God is love, and He wants to show us His love at every moment. Because God is the Alpha and the Omega, He knows the beginning from the end and the end from the beginning. Therefore, complaining is useless because He already knows how you feel and what you need before you tell or ask Him.

Secondly, we approach the Father in Jesus's name, knowing that whatever we ask in His name is already a finished work. My pastor made a statement one day that I have never forgotten. He said, "The Father wants us to have what He has already provided for us more than we want to obtain those things. Why? Because He already did it."

Thirdly, if you understand this, you will see why Jesus said do not use vain repetitions. God is not forgetful or hard of hearing. Fourthly, you don't have to beg, scream, or holler at God. Instead, find Scriptures that promise you what you are believing God for, ask once in Jesus's name, and then water that prayer with thanksgiving, knowing that God is not a man that He should lie. The prayers in this book are meant to bring knowledge and inspiration from the Scriptures. They are guides and models, not the be-all and end-all for that particular subject. We must ask the Holy Spirit to teach us how to pray, just as the disciples asked Jesus. He will teach you what to say and pray through you by His unction.

There are many types of prayer. Paul said to Timothy in 1 Timothy 2:1, "I exhort therefore that, first of all, supplications, prayers, intercessions, and giving of thanks, be made for all men." In this verse, Paul shows us four different kinds of prayer. There are more, but we will specifically focus on these four. The website "Biblical Exegete" describes supplications as entreaties.[1] This is a

---

1   Pastor Mahalon, "A Closer Look at Four Different Types of Prayer in 1 Timothy 2:1," Biblical Exegete.com, December 6, 2014, https://biblicalexegete.wordpress.com/2014/12/06/a-closer-look-at-four-different-types-of-prayer-in-1-timothy-21/.

prayer of request or a desperate prayer for one's self. We pray this prayer to God because of a "wanting need." With a supplication or entreaty, one must pray with a sense of urgency concerning their personal needs. This is a specific way of speaking to God with focused intention on things that we have to have or need now. The website "Biblical Exegete" states that "there is a tone of intentionality and expression in a supplication. You pray with a goal or an end result, which leads to purposefulness to one's prayer life. With prayers, one must pray with purpose."[2] We must learn the art of being intentional and not just praying in the dark, hoping and wishing that God will respond. If we pray blind general prayers with no aim or purpose, how will we know if God answers?

The third word, "intercession," means "petitions."[3] I heard the late Phil Halverson in a sermon called *No Limit* say that "intercessory prayer is God's love reaching out to humanity." Phil was an extraordinary intercessor in his day. He was used by God to pray for presidents and people in positions of authority. During his intercession on behalf of mankind, the Lord revealed to him many secrets that affected the world. Yes, God can use you, too, to change the world through prayer! However, unlike a supplication, intercession refers to praying specifically on behalf of another. The website "Biblical Exegete" says that it has the idea of "conversation" or "closeness."[4] The other forms of prayer could be public. But this type of prayer implies intimacy of fellowship with God. We pray "for others and bring their names and situations to God." You cannot be selfish or hateful and be an intercessor. You will instead have compassion on humanity

---

2   Ibid.

3   Ibid.

4   Ibid.

and be thankful and moved enough by their spiritual condition to pray for them.

The last type of prayer mentioned in 1 Timothy 2 is thanksgivings. When you see this word, you think of giving thanks, gratitude, and thankfulness. We cannot think of prayer as only asking God for things. Philippians 4:6 tells us, "Do not fret or have any anxiety about anything, but in every circumstance and in everything, by prayer and petition (definite requests), with thanksgiving, continue to make your wants known to God" (AMPC). The key here is to offer the prayer *with thanksgiving* to God. Paraphrasing verse 7, if we are able to do this, God's peace will be ours and we will not fear anything from Him. Instead, we will have a soul assured of its salvation, be content with our earthly lot, and have a peace that transcends all understanding mounting guard over our hearts and minds in Christ Jesus. At times, we should come to God with our only motive as praise and thanksgiving for all He has done and will continue to do in the future.

In Ephesians 6:18, Paul shared one of the greatest methods of how we can pray. He said we should be "Praying always with all prayer and supplication in the Spirit, and watching thereunto with all perseverance and supplication for all saints" (KJV). Paul refers to praying in the spirit, which is an actual place in prayer. This differs from praying in the natural or by our human understanding based on what we see. The act of prayer is a spiritual exercise of fellowshipping with God to enter His presence. We enter God's presence by and through prayer, worship, praise, and thanksgiving.

These four kinds of prayer minister to the Lord. The highest of these is praise. Let us praise and worship our heavenly Father at all times. The psalmist said in Psalm 34 to keep the Lord's praise continually in our mouths. Andrew Wommack stated in a sermon regarding prayer and titled *You Already Got It* that "95% of prayer should be thank yous for what God has already done."[5] Let's stop right now and love on Him and bless Him for all that He has done!

---

5   Andrew Wommack, "You Already Got It," August 2, 2016, sermon at Living Word Christian Center, https://www.youtube.com/watch?v=xKSuoTlFyBU.

1

THE KEY TO GREAT BIG POWER

The title of this book is *A Small Book of Prayers for Great Big Power*. Neither our effort nor our performance produces God's power. It is faith, and to have strong faith, we must have knowledge of the Word. Specifically, we need knowledge of what God has already done for us from the foundation of the world and what He did for us by sending Jesus. Ephesians 1:3–5 says, "Blessed be the God of our Lord Jesus Christ, who hath blessed us with all spiritual blessings in heavenly places in Christ: According as he hath chosen us in him before the foundation of the world that we should be holy and without blame before him in love." We must see what God *hath* already done for us before the foundation of the world to begin to understand how faith should work. Faith pulls the finished work of God from the beginning and the finished work of Christ from the cross into my current reality or condition. Foundationally speaking, we have a duality of existence with faith. The spirit realm and the natural earthly realm coexist together at the exact same time. The difference is the seen world or physical realm has to catch up with the unseen or supernatural realm or world.

Once we understand the duality of existence between the natural and spiritual realms and that God has already finished everything in the spirit, we can now begin to see how faith works to access the spirit and bring these things to the natural. The Word tells us that faith is activated and energized by love (Galatians 5:6 AMPC). Specifically, God was motivated by His love for humanity to create and provide everything we would ever need to live and survive. He made sure nothing was left out from the foundation of the world. In addition, He loved us so much that He even gave us the same measure of faith to live by that Jesus had. We see this in Galatians 2:20 where Paul said "The life [he] now lived in the flesh [he] was living by the faith of the Son of God who loved him and gave himself for him" (KJV).

With Jesus's faith, we can then see answers to prayer by activating, hearing, seeing, embracing, and receiving the promises God left for us in His Word from the beginning. We believe those promises and how God loved us in Christ Jesus on the cross in spite of the five physical senses that tell us otherwise. This moves faith from just head knowledge or a belief that God can to an intimate connection with the Father and a knowledge that He will if I believe with action. For James 2:17 tells us that "even so faith, if it hath not works, is dead, being alone."

There is a difference between faith, hope, and belief. We will discuss these differences later. But for now, faith is usually expressed when we live out our love and the love shed abroad in our hearts by the Holy Spirit toward others. The Word instructs us to look unto Jesus, the author and finisher of our faith (Hebrews 12:2). Jesus and the Father have already completed everything that we will ever need or believe. We see this in Genesis 1 when God created everything that man needed to survive in five days; then He created man in His image on the sixth day and gave him dominion over all of His creation. Genesis 1:26 shows us that man was given "complete authority over the fish of the sea, the birds of the air, the [tame] beasts, and over all of the earth, and over everything that creeps upon the earth" (AMPC). After God created man (male and female) in His own image and likeness and gave them complete authority, He rested from His (work of) creating on the seventh day. A solid understanding of this will prevent us from erroneously laboring to have and use faith. Instead, we will now labor to enter God's rest based on what He has already created, provided, and promised in His Word.

God did not leave anything out that concerns His creation. So we can take comfort knowing that God "according as his divine power hath given unto us all things that pertain unto life and godliness, through the knowledge of him that hath called us to glory and virtue: Whereby are given unto us exceeding great and precious promises: that by these [we] might be partakers of the divine nature, having escaped the corruption that is in the world through lust" (2 Peter 1:3–4).

God's love has already defeated sin and all the works of the enemy and has then placed that same power that accomplished this inside us. According to Dr. Frederick Price, we must know the following truths and realities as these are crucial to operating in faith as God intended:

- the Word of God
- the new creation or who God has made you in Christ
- your redemption when Jesus purchased your freedom from the curses of breaking God's laws
- your righteousness or the right standing God imputed to you (not earned)

☐ the indwelling Spirit or Holy Spirit, which is God living in us

☐ the authority of the name of Jesus[6]

We do not just try to accumulate or build up enough faith in order to get a response from God to do something. Rather, faith is our response to seeing and experiencing how Christ has loved us and continually hearing what that love did for us, who love or God made us, and the position of authority we have been given in Christ. For "faith comes by hearing [what is told], and what is heard comes by the preaching [of the message that came from the lips] of Christ (the Messiah Himself" (Romans 10:17 AMPC). So we must focus our attention on Jesus, keep His words, and remember the message of what He did for us and who He made us. This continuously produces faith.

It does not take a lot of effort to see the power of God work in our lives. Jesus said it only takes a mustard seed of faith or belief in Christ Jesus. (See Matthew 17:20.) Think about this. The analogy of the mustard seed to faith has nothing to do with the size of the seed or our faith being little or big. Joe Amaral shared in his book *Understanding Jesus Cultural Insights into the Words and Deeds of Christ* that when Jesus referred to the mustard seed, He was referring to its tenacity.[7] The mustard weed can be hard to kill. It can grow anywhere and usually causes everything surrounding it to taste like mustard. It has even been known to burst through concrete. Jesus wants us to operate in tenacious faith like the mustard seed and fight through everything that gets in our way.

---

6   Although the following information is from the listed author, the specific source could not be located.

7   Joe Amaral, *Understanding Jesus Cultural Insights into the Words and Deeds of Christ* (United States: FaithWords, 2011).

We have the power to take the name of Jesus and affect all that surrounds us with what He has given us.

By doing this, we can see Jesus Christ perform many miracles through us and on our behalf. When we say "Jesus Christ," "Jesus" is His name, and the word "Christ" is His title. The title "Christ" means the "Anointed One" and His anointing, which includes His power. So it takes belief in the Anointed One, Jesus, and faith in the anointing that was upon Him to see God's power work in our lives. Jesus said in Matthew 11:27 that *all* things were delivered to Him of the Father and He revealed God or made Him known to us. Jesus also told us in Luke 10:19 that He gave us His power and authority over *all* the power the enemy possesses. In addition to this, He stated that nothing shall by any means hurt us when we operate in what we have been given. This is Jesus's authority. When we believe in the power, wisdom, and goodness that God gave us through Jesus, signs and wonders will pour down on us like rain.

The key to seeing this great big power work every day is great big faith, and the key to great big faith is a great big love walk. For as we saw in Galatians 5:6, faith works by love. However, knowing that faith works by love does not tell us what faith is or how to grow it. Even though we just learned that Jesus was not talking about the size of faith when He compared it to the mustard seed, faith is still measurable. However, we measure our faith by degrees of belief and not necessarily by size. Dr. Frederick Price taught in *How Faith Works* that faith can be measured by degrees, quantities, amounts, or conditions.[8] He compiled a list of Scriptures to help people determine their faith level.

---

8   Frederick Price, *How Faith Works* (Tulsa: Harrison House, 1996).

Here are different kinds of faith you can have:

- ☐ great faith like the centurion in Matthew 8:5, who understood the power of Jesus's words

- ☐ little faith like Peter, who saw the wind in Matthew 14:22 and started doubting

- ☐ strong faith like Abraham, who was not weak in faith, considering the deadness of his and Sarah's bodies in Romans 4:19–20

- ☐ full of faith like Stephen in Acts 6:1–5

- ☐ faith that is unfeigned or sincere and not playing games in 1 Timothy 1:5

- ☐ shipwrecked faith going nowhere found in 1 Timothy 1:18–19

- ☐ wavering faith that is not consistent in James 1:5–6

- ☐ rich faith that is not poor in believing in James 2:5

- ☐ faith made perfect or mature and not infantile as seen in James 2:22

- ☐ world-overcoming faith because you are born of God as seen in 1 John 5:4

- ☐ faith growing exceedingly because your love is growing toward people as stated in 1 Thessalonians 3:12[9]

You can have a belief that God can do anything because of what He already promised in the Word, or you can live in unbelief, fear, and doubt. As previously mentioned, you sometimes know that God can perform the supernatural, but you wonder if He will do what He said in His Word for you.

---

9   Ibid.

For example, let's take a look at the story of the centurion in Matthew 8:5–13. Would Jesus say that you are great in faith like him? Jesus marveled at his great faith, because, as a Roman soldier, the centurion understood how authority worked. His faith was so great because of his belief in the power of Jesus's words. He knew the Master could just speak the word only and whatever Jesus said would happen.

This is the same faith that Jesus's mother operated in when she wanted Him to turn the water into wine in John 2:1–11. She told the men at the wedding, "Whatever He says to you, do it." I'm pretty sure when Jesus told the servants to fill up the waterpots of stone with water, they did not believe the water would turn into wine. Yet they obeyed and filled them up anyway. Jesus, on the other hand, understood how faith worked. He could see the finished work of the Father from the spirit realm and therefore accessed God's power through prayer, which resulted in water turning into wine in the natural.

When we have this kind of understanding about the power of Jesus's words, we will ask for things in prayer based on His words and promises. We will also pray and wait with expectation for Him to speak concerning our situation. Then, we will not default to fear and worry because of how things look or feel. Instead, we will have confidence to use His words to produce great power and miracles in prayer. The key to seeing answers to prayer is praying like Jesus taught us to pray in Mark 11:22–24. He told us, "Have faith in God. For verily I say unto you, That whosoever shall say unto this mountain, Be thou removed, and be thou cast into the sea; and shall not doubt in his heart, but shall believe that those things which he saith shall come to pass; he shall have whatsoever he saith. Therefore, I say unto you, What things soever ye desire, when ye pray, believe that ye receive them, and ye shall have them." Joe Amaral taught in *Understanding Jesus Cultural Insights into the Words and Deeds of Christ,* that the mountains that Jesus references here are authority figures. Jewish leaders were called mountains and would often say my mountain will crush your mountain, concerning certain viewpoints related to Scripture.[10] In light of this knowledge, we can see that Jesus was teaching that we have to speak to the authority figures sent by the enemy and tell them to be removed from our lives and cast into the sea.

Practically speaking, if the enemy brings a sickness, depression, or anything else that's not from Jesus and his finished work on the cross, I am to tell it to be removed. Jesus taught as one who was and is authority. Therefore, He is the final authority on every situation and case that we will face in this life. We also have to believe by trusting and being confident. We believe that we receive what we are praying for. Jesus was teaching that what we desire when praying in faith should be received by faith at the moment we pray and not later. Also, we must be diligent and consistent to thank God for what He has already done, and then we will see it happen if we don't doubt in our hearts. We do this before we see anything occur. To understand being consistent and persistent, we need to look at the story of the widow and the unjust judge in Luke 18:1–8.

This parable teaches us to pray always and not to turn coward, faint, lose heart, or give up in prayer. Most people give up based on what they hear or because of how the situation looks or feels. The widow in this parable was very persistent and focused about receiving justice against her adversary. She was so persistent that

---

10   Amaral, *Understanding.*

even a judge who did not fear God or man gave her justice for her husband because she continued to bother him. The Amplified Bible Classic Edition stated that she gave the judge "intolerable annoyance" and would have worn him out by her continual coming. The judge stated that he had better give her what she wanted or she would assault him.

After sharing this parable of persistence in the natural, Jesus then told the disciples to listen to what the unjust judge stated but then showed them how God really is in verse 7. Jesus said that "[Our just] God defend[s] and protect[s] and avenge[s] His elect (His chosen ones), who cry to Him day and night." He asked a question next about God, saying, "Will He defer them and delay help on their behalf?" The answer lies in verse 8 when Jesus shows us the character and heart of God by saying, "He will defend and protect and avenge [us] speedily. However, when the Son of Man comes, will He find [persistence in] faith on the earth?" (AMPC). Sometimes, we need to persist in faith or in believing the finished work of creation and the cross. Do you cry out to God day and night until you receive your answers to prayer?

I wonder what would have happened to Daniel in Daniel 9 if he would have given up in prayer. Verse 23 says, "As soon as you [he (Daniel)] began to make your [his (Daniel's)] request, a reply was sent" (GOD'S WORD). The angel Gabriel came to Daniel directly to give him an answer to his prayer. He stated, "I have come to give you the reply because you are highly respected. So study the message and understand the vision" (vs. 23 GOD'S WORD). The angel Gabriel did not reach Daniel with an answer to his prayer for twenty-one days. Gabriel told Daniel that, as soon as he had prayed, God had sent him with the answer. However, in Daniel 10, the angel told him, "Don't be afraid, Daniel. God has heard everything that you said ever since the first day you decided to humble yourself in front of your God so that you could learn to understand things. I have come in response to your prayer. The commander of the Persian kingdom opposed me for 21 days. But then Michael, one of the chief commanders, came to help me because I was left alone with the kings of Persia" (GOD'S WORD).

The only difference with us is that we do not have to wait for God to come down and bring us an answer because He lives in us. But sometimes we do have to persist because our adversary tries to block, hinder, delay, and slow down the things of God. If we don't quit believing, speaking, confessing, and thanking God for His exceeding great and precious promises in prayer, we will see them come to pass. The Holy Spirit will give us insight into why things are working or not working in prayer. We must seek Him for answers and not give up!

The Bible actually says in 1 John 2:20 that "[we] have an unction from the Holy One, and [we] know all things." This verse refers to "all things," which we don't know with head knowledge or in the natural realm, but in the spirit realm because of the Holy Spirit that was poured out on us and in us by Jesus.

However, we must learn the art and discipline of persisting in faith when we do not immediately see the physical manifestation of the prayer. Our heavenly Father already wants to give us what we ask for in prayer when it aligns with His Word. He has already done everything for us in Christ Jesus. Jesus's last words on the cross were recorded in John 19:30. "It is finished." This means that everything we seek or ask God for has already been provided for us through Christ. Just as when God sent the answer to prayer for Daniel the first time that he prayed, He sends our answer the first time that we pray. However, we may have to persist and do battle with evil spirits who try to hold up our answers. This is why we cannot give up when we pray. We must continue until we see God answer. Angels could be battling on your behalf right now because of a prayer that you previously prayed. They are fueled on by our continued and persistent prayer, worship, and praise. Our words have great power.

God already sees the finished work that Jesus completed on the cross. Therefore, we approach God as though the work is already done and not as if we are trying to get Him to do something. But just because the work of the cross is a finished work, we do not automatically have the victory of the cross working for us daily. When we have an understanding of Jesus's finished work, we will walk in total victory without defeat every single day. This means we win, no matter the test or the trial that we experience. We must enforce Jesus's victory by believing in His message and speaking His promises to the Father in prayer. Sometimes we have to speak to Satan and his demons with power and authority from Jesus. For Jesus already took stripes on His back so that we could be healed, made whole, saved, set free, and delivered with His peace and joy. Peace means to be complete and whole in every way. Again, it takes faith to believe that what you are praying for is already done.

In order to really understand what praying in faith entails, we need to look at Hebrews 11:1 and Romans 10:17 again in the Amplified Bible Classic Edition. A lot of people think they are praying in faith. However, I have found over the years that people are not really praying in faith. Rather, they might be praying nice prayers without much spiritual or scriptural substance. God said that His Word would not return to Him void when it is prayed in faith. (See Isaiah 55:11.) Void is a dark and empty place that cannot produce. God's Word, when it is sown in faith on good ground, will always produce a good harvest. What kind of harvest will you receive? It will be a harvest of whatever words you have sown in the Spirit by believing and speaking God's promises. If you meditate on or sow healing verses, you will reap a harvest of divine health. If you sow prosperity verses, you will reap a harvest of financial stability. Furthermore, this will work in any area where you take the time to believe God's Word. We must find Scriptures that promise us what we are believing God for in prayer.

People often ask, "Why don't people get the answers to what they are believing God for in prayer?" The answer lies in asking if we truly have a firm belief and relying trust that God's Word is true. Are we really convinced that God cannot lie? The Merriam-Webster Dictionary says the word "relying" means to be dependent on something.[11] Further, it means to have confidence based on experience. How many experiences have you had with God performing miracles? Have you ever been inspired by someone else's experience or testimony about what God has done for them? Have you had enough experiences with God from testimonies to fully trust Him with total confidence? If you are not convinced that what God said in His Word is true and that circumstances can lie, then you will not come to God with confidence and boldness. If you do not have confidence in prayer, then you cannot pray from a position of faith. When we are praying from a position of faith, we are guaranteed to get results every time.

---

11   *Merriam-Webster,* s.v., "rely (*n.*)," accessed March 4, 2020, https://www.merriam-webster.com/dictionary/rely.

On the other hand, if we do not have confidence or pray from a position of faith, we will not see the power of God at work in our everyday lives. Instead of faith, most people pray in a posture of hope, fear, doubt, or unbelief. These four areas will rob the child of God of receiving answers from Him in prayer. You cannot have confidence in God when you are afraid, hoping, wishing, or even doubting that God can perform His word. God can and will perform His word in your life when you believe. Let's look further into these four areas of hope, fear, doubt, and unbelief. We need to see what it means to pray in each of these four danger zones.

First, we see the word hope. Bible-believing hope is an expectation about what God will do in the future while faith is an expectation for what will happen right now. The Merriam-Webster Dictionary defines hope as a desire that you cherish with anticipation, expectation of obtainment or fulfillment.[12] It is to want something to happen or to be true. When one is hoping, they are expecting something with confidence. Hope is necessary, and we should never lose hope. However, even though it is not wrong to have hope, we must move past believing what God can do in the future to what He already did for us on the cross. Kenneth Hagin taught in a message called *What Faith Is* that "faith gives substance to the things that we hope for.[13] You have to be confident of what you hope for and be convinced of what you don't see. Hope does not have any substance by itself. You never hope for what you possess" because you already have it. So when you don't have something, you need hope. Because of the sacrifice that Jesus

---

12   *Merriam-Webster*, s.v., "hope (*n.*)," accessed July 31, 2020, https://www.merriam-webster.com/dictionary/hope.

13   Although the following information is from the listed author, the specific source could not be located.

made for us on the cross, I can receive that work as mine right now. Again, God's work in Christ is a finished work.

So if it is already done, then it is available to me right now. Therefore, I should not have to wait to receive what He has promised. I believe I receive what Jesus did for me on the cross *right now*. When I read or hear a promise of God in the Word, it feeds my faith and causes me to believe because faith comes by hearing. But when I begin to confess it over and over and say that I believe I receive it now, the truth gets down into my spirit and manifests in my body. This becomes my point of contact, and I move from a place of hoping, wishing, thinking, fearing, and doubting to a place of joy in believing and speaking, which causes miracles to manifest.

Secondly, a great monster called fear attacks our faith. I heard Kenneth Copeland preach that "fear tolerated is faith contaminated."[14] For fear is faith, but in the wrong thing. Instead of the faith being rooted in the promises God gave us in His Word, this faith will stem from negative reports, bad situations, feelings, emotions, and evil spirits. Understand that "God ha[s] not given us the spirit of fear; but of power, and of love, and of a sound mind" (2 Timothy 1:7). Fear is a spirit that lies and distorts facts and realities into scary unknown balls of chaos and mess.

Therefore, the acronym for fear is "False Evidence Appearing Real (F.E.A.R.)."[15] If you have an expectation of danger or an evil foreboding, you are in a form of fear. Fear carries with it the thought or a feeling that the future might not turn out well for

---

14   Kenneth Copeland, *Break the Chain of Worry: The Joy of Living a Carefree Life* (Tulsa: Harrison House, 2016).

15   The acronym has been around for years and is commonly used. As such, a specific attribution could not be located.

me. As Christians, we should never allow this spirit to operate in our thinking. If you do not deal with the spirit of fear, it will paralyze you so that you cannot move or function in life. But 1 John 4:18 says that perfect love casts out fear. When we know how much the Father in heaven loves us and what that love has done for us on the cross, His love and power will expel every trace of terror and fear from danger forever.

On the other hand, doubt and unbelief are expectations that God will not hear or respond. Doubt and unbelief question the ability or the existence of God. Doubt causes you to live your life full of questions and confusion. This person will hear the promises of God and then wonder if He can perform them. They may even feel that they have to do everything right for God to hear and respond to them in prayer. However, God put everything in Jesus who never did anything wrong. So even if we miss it or sin, we can come to Jesus to receive forgiveness and be washed in His blood. Then, we can still believe that God will hear and answer our prayers as though sin has never been. You can rebuke doubt and tell it to get out of your thinking in Jesus's name. You can also remove doubt and unbelief by feeding on the Word of God and reading it daily. The only cure for unbelief is to believe.

You do not need forgiveness of this enemy to our faith. Instead, you must make a firm decision to believe that what God said in His Word is the absolute truth. Any outside voice talking to our minds that is not in agreement with what Jesus taught, said, and did for us on the cross is coming from the wicked one. Those thoughts must be taken captive, cast down, brought into the obedience of Christ, and the spirits associated with those voices must be resisted in the name of Jesus. If we resist and refuse to believe what those voices are saying, they will flee from us.

The goal of this book is to help the believer petition God through prayer and navigate from a position of faith instead of from one these four danger zones. There is a huge difference. God does not answer prayers because of our strivings to be good or right based on formulas, rules, regulations, prayers, Bible reading, or even our mistakes, but rather because of love and belief. We must ask ourselves, "How are we actually approaching God when praying?" Now that we have a clear understanding of what faith is not, we can explore what faith is and how we can obtain it if we do not already have it.

2

WHAT IS FAITH AND HOW DO WE KEEP IT ACTIVATED?

Gloria Copeland taught in her healing school and as quoted on social media that "faith is the resource, the power, the ability to receive the supernatural ability of God in your spirit, in your soul, in your body, and the circumstances of life. Faith changes every situation when applied, and it gives freedom from the curse of poverty, disease, turmoil, and sadness." This shows us that a force is working in the spirit of faith. Further, Hebrews 11:1 gives us a very clear definition of faith. "*Now* faith is the assurance (the confirmation, the title deed) of the things [we] hope for, being the proof of things [we] do not see and the conviction of their reality [faith perceiv[es], as a real fact, what is not revealed to the senses]"(AMPC, emphasis added). Faith is a spiritual force and can be a seed of God's word planted with words from the believers' mouth into our hearts or into the atmosphere. Faith is acting on what you believe, and it is released by words through your mouth. You only believe until you see the manifestation of that which you believe for. Once you have it, you no longer need to believe. This is why faith is the evidence of what I do not see. So faith has nothing to do with using your common sense to figure things out. You only have to believe what God said in His Word and do not need to believe your five physical senses. When you focus on the words that came from Jesus's lips, your faith will stay activated and at work in your life.

Faith and belief differ from each other. Faith acts on the finished promises of God, while belief will know the promises of God are true but never act on them to do anything with them. Belief can be sincere in knowing God's promises are the truth, but just knowing the promises does not put them into action. Therefore, belief alone can never be faith. Belief can also be twisted by the five physical senses if the believer is not sober in their thinking or focused on the truth only found in Christ Jesus.

The five physical senses are what you can see, touch, hear, feel, smell, and taste. If you live by your five physical senses, you will have a lot of trouble in life because your senses can lie to you. They are usually not the truth that we see in the Scriptures. The devil will make sure that what you see and hear distracts you from faith. Satan loves to trigger or ignite people into unbelief by keeping them in their feelings and emotions and not in faith. The Holy Spirit helps us live out of our spirit man or in faith and not out of our thoughts or emotions. It behooves me to emphasize here that "whatsoever is not of faith is sin" (Romans 14:23). So living by faith and not out of our heads is very important to the Lord.

When we are living from our soul, we are living from our mind, will, and emotions, which the Bible says are carnal. A carnal mind lives by the five physical senses or the flesh and is not controlled by the Holy Spirit. Romans 8:6 states, "To be carnally minded is death; but to be spiritually minded is life and peace." We must have the mind of Christ or the Holy Spirit to be successful in prayer.

We have to remember that we are a spirit being with a spirit, a soul, and a body. We should be activating all three. The spirit man, which is the real you, is the part that is recreated in Christ Jesus when we are born again or saved. We contact God with our spirit, not our head. As I mentioned, your soul is your mind, your will, and your emotions. We are told in the Bible to "renew our minds with the washing of the water of the word" (Ephesians 5:26). Practically, we do this by reading the Bible, which helps replace old ways of thinking with fresh, new, and positive thoughts about the impossible or the supernatural. James 1:21 instructs you to "receive with meekness the engrafted word which is able to save your souls [or your thinking]." Yes, reading the Bible saves us from thinking crazy thoughts. Remember, we have to be focused and intentional with purpose when praying. Our minds cannot be loose and running wild with thoughts all over the place and still be effective in prayer. Reign in those thoughts and make them obey Jesus.

Next, we have the body to deal with in keeping faith going. The Word of God instructs us to keep our body under submission in 1 Corinthians 9:27. This means to not let the body rule and control who you are and what you do. Further, another synonym in the Bible for the body is the flesh. It is also called a godless human nature without the Holy Spirit. The flesh never likes being told what to do in life. We must learn to put our body, flesh, or godless human nature under the control of the human spirit and Holy Spirit. We cannot let the body or the flesh rule and dominate us by telling us what to do every day. The flesh will try to rule by fighting to have its own way. It only cares about what makes it feel good, and it fights the mind and spirit to please the physical senses. It does not submit itself to God or to His standards. Therefore, it is hostile to God, meaning it is filled with hatred toward Him. As such, you will never receive anything from God when you allow yourself to be dominated by what He hates. So if we want to receive answers to prayer, we must submit to God's prescribed way of reaching or contacting Him through our spirit man. We must stay in the Spirit to have the victory in prayer. From this explanation, we can see that if we are ruled by the carnal mind, we will never be in a place of faith to see miracles, signs, and wonders transpire.

This is why Romans 10:17 is so important in understanding further what true faith actually is and what it is not. True faith is definitely not just a nice, general prayer. It is very specific. This verse says that "faith comes by hearing what is told, and what is heard comes by the preaching of the message that came from the lips of Christ (the Messiah Himself)" (AMPC). From this verse, we can see that Jesus's words are faith, and this belief in the impossible will come when we hear His words. If you are praying Jesus's red words found in Matthew, Mark, Luke, and John, then you will truly know that you are praying in faith, and you will have the right foundation upon which to build when you read the letters and the rest of the New Testament. Jesus's teachings are explained further in the letters. The teachings in the Gospels help you understand what is written in the letters. You must find Scriptures in the Bible that promise you what you are believing God for. If you don't find Scriptures to stand on, believe, and speak when you pray, you cannot have confidence that God will hear and answer your prayers. He only responds to His Word. Remember, He said that His Word will not return to Him void.

We can't allow the devil to steal our confidence in God's ability and power to do the impossible on our behalf. Hebrews 10:35 says to "cast not away therefore your confidence, which hath great recompense of reward." In addition, Hebrews 10:23 encourages us to "hold fast to the profession of our hope without wavering; (for he is faithful that promised)." Therefore, we can't let our enemy make us doubt God's ability or power. The Lord is a rewarder of those that diligently seek Him, according to Hebrews 11:6. Webster's dictionary describes the word "diligent" as a "steady, earnest, and energetic effort."[16] It says your effort can even be painstaking. Let's be diligent about seeking our miracle-working God today. However, along with your diligence, you must be sure to have patience.

James 1:2–8 teaches us to count it *all* joy when we encounter different temptations. It also admonishes us to let patience have her perfect work. Patience is when we stay the same, no matter what happens. This describes Jesus perfectly. Hebrews 13:8 says, "Jesus Christ the same yesterday, today, and forever." We need patience when we pray so that we don't give up, faint, or lose heart if we do not see the answer right away.

We have to learn to stay consistent in prayer and stand our ground on the promises of God, in spite of how the situation may look or feel. This includes counting it all joy and staying the same when envy or strife is present so that we will not be in every evil work. James 3:16 says that "where envying and strife is, there is confusion and every evil work" (KJV). We can't let these monsters deactivate our faith. So if the situation appears to worsen, we must stay the same or in patience to see the reward or

16   *Merriam-Webster*, s.v., "diligent (*adj.*)," accessed March 4, 2020, https://www.merriam-webster.com/dictionary/diligent.

fruit from our faith. Don't forget that God is a rewarder of those who diligently seek Him. God has answered our prayers before the foundation of the world. The moment we pray, when we believe that we receive, we access what God has already done. So even though you may not see changes or answers right away, sometimes we just have to stand on the Word and not budge.

James also tells us that when we ask God for something, we should ask "in faith" with nothing wavering. If you waver, you are hesitant or doubting. The Bible says that the man who thinks this way will not receive anything from God. This is why Paul urges us in Romans 12:3 "not to think of ourselves more highly than we ought to think; but to think soberly, according as God hath dealt to every man the measure of faith" (KJV). To think soberly is to think only one way and not in a double-minded fashion. A double-minded person is considered to be someone with two minds. One part of the mind believes that God can do anything; the other part questions and doubts the existence of God and if He will actually perform His Word. You can't receive from God unless you are single-minded and convinced Jesus can and will do something about what you are bringing to Him in prayer. God made sure He gave us the tools to defeat this mindset by giving us the measure of the God kind of faith.

Sometimes people struggle to believe that God will hear and answer their prayers. They feel as though they do not have enough faith or they have too much sin for God to listen to them. They don't really understand how much God loves them and what that love has already done for them on the cross by defeating everything that is wrong in their lives. However, God has given each of us exactly the same measure of faith that Jesus had. He loved us enough to give us a measure of Himself so that we would have no deficiency in our believing. We must believe in the love God has and wants to show to His children. We must not only receive God's love by faith, but we must also be willing to walk in it and give it away to others. These are all important as they relate to getting answers to prayer and keeping our faith working properly.

Faith works by love, and love is the key to a successful prayer life. Therefore, we must walk in love so that our prayers are not hindered and we aren't cut off without access to God, who is love. Take a moment and meditate on what Paul wrote in Ephesians 3:14–20. He stated that he would bow his knees to Jesus so that Christ could "dwell in our hearts by faith" (v. 17). He wanted Christ through our faith "to [actually] dwell (settle down, abide, make His permanent home) in our hearts." He wanted us to be "rooted deep in love and founded securely on love." Then we could have "power and be strong to apprehend and grasp with all the saints [God's devoted people, the experience of that love] what is the breadth and length and height and depth [of it]." He wanted us to "[really come] to know [practically, through experience for ourselves] the love of Christ, which far surpasses mere knowledge [without experience]" and to "be filled [through all our being] unto all the fullness of God." Then, we could have "the richest measure of love's divine Presence, and become a body wholly filled and flooded with God Himself!" Now, we are in a position to see the result of living in a full measure of God's love. Paul said, "Now to Him Who, by (in consequence of) the [action of His] power that is at work within us, is able to [carry out His purpose and] do superabundantly, far over and above all that we [dare] ask or think [infinitely beyond our highest prayers, desires, thoughts, hopes, or dreams] (AMPC).

Throughout that passage of Scripture, you can see how important it is to walk in love. Through love, you will see God go beyond what you could ever ask, think, pray, or desire. But if you stay angry with people and don't walk in love, Satan will destroy your ability to receive from God. Further, in Mark 11:26, the Lord said, "If you do not forgive others, then you will not be forgiven." When a person remains in a state of unforgiveness, they are working against what Jesus did for us on the cross.

According to Romans 5:8, Jesus loved the whole world while we were yet sinners. A person cannot expect to receive from God, who is love, when they refuse to forgive. We are told God is love in 1 John 4:16. First Peter 4:8 says that "love or God covers a multitude of sins," and Romans 2:4 says that it is "the goodness of God that leads us to repentance." When God is good to us even when we are wrong, we will want to please Him by doing what is right in return. God's goodness, when we don't deserve it, will make us cry at times. You are truly walking in love when you can love a person while they are still a sinner or different from you.

Lastly, let's make sure that we are submitted to God, who is love, so that we can resist the devil and watch him flee from us. In other words, if we want to be able to pray and stop the works of the enemy dead in his tracks, then we need to be under love's rule and control. When we are under love's rule, we can make the enemy and his demons flee or run away from us. According to James 4:7, we must submit ourselves to God. Then we can resist the devil, and he will flee from us. We will terrorize devils when we are submitted to God. We must come under God's rule, control, and authority. No one else can do this for us. We must bow our own knees to Jesus's lordship. God is a gentleman and will never force Himself on us. We choose Him, knowing He knows the future and already has everything worked out on our behalf. God is love, so we are submitting ourselves to love's way of doing and being right in Christ Jesus. We can always trust love. God will never forsake us or leave us as an orphan in a helpless state. He knows the beginning from the end and the end from the beginning. This is why we want to yield to His rule. He knows the end result, so we can relax and trust Him to work things out.

The power of prayer is an amazing force on this earth. The disciples asked Jesus to teach them how to pray in Matthew 6:9–13. When He taught them the Lord's Prayer, He taught them that they could have things on the earth in the same way as God has things in heaven. Yes, praying brings a piece of heaven to earth. Nothing happens in this natural earthly realm until it happens in the heavenly, spiritual, unseen world first. We need to be like the disciples and ask Jesus to teach us how to pray. When we do that, the Holy Spirit will come to our aid and teach us all things.

When the Holy Spirit teaches us to pray, He will show us Galatians 3:13. This verse of Scripture tells us that "God hath redeemed us from the curse of breaking God's laws." Everything that we face that is evil can be summed up in three areas: separation from God's blessed influence; sicknesses and diseases; and the curse of poverty. If you want to see the full list of what Christ has delivered you from, read the entire chapter of Deuteronomy 28. As you read, remember that Jesus became a curse for us so that we don't have to suffer like the world or people who have no covenant with God. The word "hath" is a past tense word in this passage, which means that our redemption is already done or finished. The word "redeemed" means that Jesus purchased our freedom from the penalty of not obeying God's laws. Romans 6:23 says that the wage of sin is death. A wage is a penalty or paycheck of death or whatever God is not. The paycheck comes as a result of disobeying God's standards of righteousness or way of doing and being right in Jesus. Sin opens the door for the curse to work in our lives. Sin also causes us to receive a bad paycheck instead of the blessings God wants us to have. Learn to close the door on sin.

God does not bring a bad paycheck. Jesus taught in John 10:10 that the thief (Satan) came to steal, kill, and destroy. But Jesus came that we might have life and that we might have it more abundantly. According to the Amplified Version Classic Edition, Jesus came for us to have life in abundance to the full until it overflows. Jesus and God are one. Colossians 1:15 states that Christ is the visible image of the invisible God. If Jesus wanted us to have life in abundance, then God wants the same thing. Jesus let us know in John 14:10 that He never said anything of His own authority or of His own accord. But the Father who lived in Jesus was doing the works we saw in His ministry through Him. Christ wants to come and live in us so that He can do God's mighty works through us. We can then truly walk in freedom from curses.

When Christians begin to understand who they are in Christ and the power that they have been given as Christians, they will not be limited to what they ask God for in prayer. Jesus put it this way in Mark 9:23. "All things are possible to those who believe." First John 3:23 says that "whatsoever we ask, we receive of him, because we keep his commandments, and do those things that are pleasing in his sight." Therefore, I encourage every Christian to do what is right in the Lord's sight so that you can receive whatsoever you ask.

Remember to find Scriptures that promise you what you are believing God for. The Scriptures will accomplish what pleases God, and they will prosper in what they were sent to accomplish, according to Isaiah 55:11. Let's put the Word of God to work today.

3

PRAYERS FOR DIRECTION

Psalm 25:4–5; 37:23; 119:30; Proverbs 14:12; Jeremiah 29:11; Matthew 6:33; John 16:13; 1 Corinthians 10:13; 12:28; 15:33; Galatians 6:9; Ephesians 1:17; 2:10; Philippians 1:9–10; Colossians 1:9; 2 Thessalonians 3:5; 2 John 1:9; Jude 1:24

My Notes:

Oral Roberts taught people to expect a miracle every day and even wrote a book about how to do it. If you are not expecting miracles, then you are not expecting answers to your prayers. To see real results in prayer, our prayers must be Spirit-led. The Holy Spirit will direct us to the heart of the Father and pray the perfect will of God through us if we ask Him.

When you pray for direction, you should expect the Holy Spirit to teach, lead, and guide you into God's purposes, plans, and pursuits for your life. Jeremiah 29:11 says that God "knows the plans He has for us . . . plans to prosper us and not to harm us, plans to give us hope and a future." So we need to seek God's way of doing and being right in Jesus.

That means that we can never want our own way in life. We have to seek God's rule and His righteousness in us as believers on this earth. This puts us in a position for God to add whatever we need along the way. We want God to lead, guide, and rule us because He knows the past, present, and future, and His plans for us are good and not evil. His rule will tell us what to do, what to say, how to act, and where to go. Doing things His way will cause us to live in love, peace, and joy, with victory on every side.

Prayer:

Lord, I am expecting a miracle today. We believe and speak that something good is going to happen to us today as You show us what to do and where to go. Take our lives and do something good with them.

Thank You, Lord, that You're a miracle-working God and my Creator. Thank You, Lord, for the Holy Spirit who gives me wisdom from heaven to make the right decisions. I allow Him to tell me what to do in life. You said that His job was to lead and guide me into all truth. You said that He also gives me Your message and announces to me what will happen in the future. Therefore, Lord, I choose Your way of faithfulness by setting Your rules before me and allowing the Holy Spirit to lead and guide me. Thank You that I am filled and controlled with the knowledge of Your will when I listen to and obey the Holy Spirit. Holy Spirit, I pray that You give me wisdom and spiritual understanding concerning the Father's plans, purposes, and pursuits for right now and in the future.

I need You, Holy Spirit, to assist me, to help me, to teach me, and to bring all things back to my remembrance that You have taught me in the Word. Give me a greater hunger and thirst for You. Help me to truly come under Your rule so that I may see God's covenant established on this earth and have everything Jesus provided and added to me. Thank You for Your peace and understanding. Lord, I have perfect peace when I am following the direction You have given me by the Holy Spirit. I give You all the glory and honor in Jesus's name.

Lord, help me to be sharp and prompt today to obey the voice of Jesus, the Good Shepherd. Don't let me obey or follow the voices of evil spirits who want to take me away from Your path. I choose to yield to Your plans, purposes, and pursuits. I bow down to Your lordship, Jesus. I am going after what You want me to go after in this life. I thank You, Lord, for the good life that You have made ready for me to live on this earth. Holy Spirit, show me how and what God has prearranged for me to live.

Lord, direct my heart into Your love and into the patient waiting for Christ. I pray that my love would abound more and more in knowledge and in all judgment. I want to approve what is excellent so that I can be sincere and without offense until the day of Christ. Help me to sense what is vital and do only that. Don't let me become weary in well-doing. For You said I would reap if I did not faint from continually doing what is right.

Lord, we thank You that You do not lead us into temptation, but You lovingly deliver us from evil. Thank You for continuously leading, guiding, and helping us not to sadden or vex the Holy Spirit whom You sent to represent Jesus and act on His behalf. We know that we can grieve the Holy Spirit through crazy words that we are speaking that are not Jesus's words or by not walking in love. Therefore, help us to speak faith-filled words and to stay out of strife.

Also, help us not to disregard the teachings of Christ but to put them into practice in our everyday lives. Open the Scriptures to us, Holy Spirit, make them alive and explain them to us so that we can live them to the fullest without mistakes. You said through every temptation that You would give us a way of escape. Thank You, Lord, that we see our way of escape in every temptation and we take it.

Father, I give You praise, glory, and honor for being my miracle-working God and Creator. Thank You that You are the glory and lifter of my head. Thank You for the plan You have given us on this earth. Help me to use it to declare the name of Jesus boldly. In Jesus's name.

Father, I hunger and thirst for Your righteousness, and You promised, Lord, that I would be filled. I am seeking first Your kingdom and Your righteousness. Thank You, Lord, for ruling me as a believer on this earth. I want Your way of doing and being right. Thank You, Holy Spirit, for keeping me from stumbling, slipping, and falling in life.

Thank You for the people and the order that You have established in the church and in my life to help lead, guide, and teach me. Lord, I know that evil communications can corrupt good manners, morals, and character. Therefore, thank You, Lord, for keeping me from being deceived and misled by contaminating influences. Guide me and show me how to overcome evil with good.

Lord, thank You for revealing Your Word to me and continuing to teach me the Scriptures as I seek You. Thank You for wisdom and knowledge to make the right decisions. Thank You for giving me the knowledge of the truth that's in Christ Jesus. Because of this knowledge, I can now discern between who is doing what in my life. Lord, give me the wisdom to know clearly what You are doing, what the thief is doing, and what I am supposed to do in response to both. For You said in Your Word that there are ways that seem right to men, but that way is the way of death. I allow You to lead me to the way of life and peace.

Thank You, Lord, for making me a good person. For a good person's steps are ordered by You, oh Lord, and You delight in their way. Lord, I love You so much and thank You for this day. I give You praise, glory, and honor in Jesus's name. Amen.

4

PRAYERS FOR REINFORCING YOUR POWER

Isaiah 54:17; Mark 11:22–26: Luke 10:19; John 10:5, 10; 14:14; 15:7; Acts 1:8; Ephesians 1:17; 6:10–18; Philippians 3:10, Colossians 2:15; 1 John 3:8; Revelation 12:11

My Notes:

The Merriam-Webster Dictionary describes "power" as the "ability to move with great speed or force."[17] It is physical might, possession of control, authority, or influence over others. When you have power, you have the ability to act or produce an effect on something.

The Bible says in Acts 1:8 that "you shall receive power, after that the Holy Ghost has come upon you." However, God does not just give us His power with no purpose. The second part of that verse says that the power comes so that we could become bold witnesses in the world. Jesus also taught in Luke 10:19 that He gave us power. Specifically, He stated, "Behold! I have given you authority and power to trample upon serpents and scorpions, and [physical and mental strength and ability] over all the power that the enemy [possesses]; and nothing shall in any way harm

---

17   *Merriam-Webster,* s.v., "power (*n.*)," accessed March 4, 2020, https://www. merriam-webster.com/dictionary/power.

you" (AMPC). When Jesus said "behold," He wants you to pay close attention to what He was about to say. We should know that we have specific power that has been given to us.

The first power mentioned in Luke 10:19 means you have God's *dunamis* power. The word refers to strength, power, and ability and is the root word from our English words "dynamite," "dynamo," and "dynamic."[18] When God gives us dunamis, it is not just any kind of power. It is a specific power for the miraculous and for marvelous works to take place. The Got Questions website indicates that the Greek word dunamis is used 120 times in the New Testament.[19]

"Power" means "ability the second time it is mentioned in Luke 10:19.[20] God gives us His ability over all the works that the enemy could even attempt. This power or authority is delegated power. This means that you cannot earn it and you don't deserve it. It is given to us, and the source that is backing us up when we operate in it is Almighty God Himself. This is not our own power, but rather God's power working through us to do for us what we cannot do for ourselves.

Prayer:

Thank You, Lord, that I am strong in You and in the power of Your might. Thank You for the whole armor of God that helps me stand against the wiles of the devil. Your armor is protecting my mind with the helmet of salvation and my loins with the truth

---

18   Bible hub.com, "Luke 10:19, 'power,'" accessed March 4, 2020, https://biblehub.com/luke/10-19.htm.

19   "What Is the Meaning of the Greek Word *dunamis* in the Bible?" Got Questions.com, accessed March 4, 2020, https://www.gotquestions.org/dunamis-meaning.html.

20   "Power," https://biblehub.com/luke/10-19.htm.

of Jesus's words. I put on the breastplate of righteousness and integrity and shod my feet with the gospel of peace. Lord, help me to take the shield of faith in Your love to quench all the fiery darts of the wicked one. I take the sword of the Spirit, which is Your Word, and I pray always with all prayer and supplication in the Spirit.

Lord, don't let Satan teach me. I hear Your voice, and the voice of a stranger or the evil one, I will not follow. Thank You, Jesus, that You were sent to loosen, dissolve, and destroy the works the devil has done in my family, church, and country. Thank You, Lord, that the eyes of my understanding are enlightened that I may know the hope to which You have called me. Help me see what the exceeding greatness of Your power is for me as a believer. Help me operate in the highest level of Your power. Lord Jesus, help me to know You, the power of Your resurrection, and the fellowship of Your sufferings so that I may be conformed to You in every way.

Thank You, Lord, for a spirit of wisdom and revelation in the knowledge of who You are. You're a good Father and a God of restoration. I thank You that the same power that raised Jesus from the dead is working in me. I pray for wisdom for my family, how to use what I've been given through Christ Jesus, and how to make the enemy stop and flee. Father, I love You, and I am so grateful for Your Word and that the entrance of Your Word brings light to dark places. Thank You that Your Word has the power to transform me in my spirit, soul, and body. Thank You, Lord, that I will never be the same in Jesus's name. I am constantly being transformed into the image of Your Son.

Lord Jesus, You told me in Mark 11 that I had the power to speak to mountains and command things to be removed and cast into the sea. I command _____ to be removed from my life and/or body now in Jesus's name. No weapon formed against me shall prosper in Jesus's name. I plead the blood of Jesus over my life and all that concerns me. I am made free, and I overcome everything the enemy brings against me by the blood of the Lamb and the word of my testimony. I thank You, Lord, that You have disarmed every principality and power that was ranged or joined in an attack against me in Jesus's name. I now mock them and make a show of them openly, as You did on the cross for me. Amen.

5

PRAYERS FOR FREEDOM FROM ADDICTIONS

Psalm 23:1; Psalm 50:15; Matthew 13:7; Mark 11:22–25; John 8:12, 31–32; 14:14; 15:7; Romans 12:2; 1 Corinthians 10:13–14; 15:33; Galatians 3:13; Colossians 2:15; Philippians 2:5; Hebrews 13:8; 1 John 2:16;3:20; 5:21

My Notes:

The Merriam-Webster Dictionary describes an addiction as a compulsive, chronic, physiological or psychological need for a habit-forming substance, behavior, or activity having harmful physical, psychological, or social effects and typically causing well-defined symptoms (such as anxiety, irritability, tremors, or nausea) upon withdrawal or abstinence. The state of being addicted is a strong inclination to do, use, or indulge in something repeatedly. In the same manner, a lust is a very strong craving or desire for something.[21] The desire can be intense and create a longing for what is desired. Most people only think of lust as it relates to feelings of sexual desire or idolatry. However, 1 John 5:21 says, "Little children, keep yourselves from idols (false gods)-[from anything and everything that would occupy the place in your heart due to God, from any sort of substitute for

---

21   *Merriam-Webster*, s.v., "lust (*n.*)," accessed March 4, 2020, https://www.merriam-webster.com/dictionary/lust.

Him that would take first place in your life]" (AMPC).

You can have a very strong desire for many things. Therefore, lust can be either good or bad. When we have a very strong desire to please the Father, we are on the right track. But if we have an uncontrollable urge to please the flesh in any way, it may cross over into being an addiction, and then there will be trouble.

Remember, Satan desires to control people's minds so that he can control their bodies. He wants them addicted to sin and darkness with no way out. He will control them because of their lust. James 1:14 says, "each man is tempted when he is carried away and enticed by his own lust" (NASB 1977). A lust unchecked and pulling you in the wrong direction is an open door for the enemy to take over your life through an addiction. However, the Lord also desires and longs for us to have a strong desire for Him so that He can rule our minds and bodies as well. Imagine being addicted to Jesus. He said if we continued in His word, we would be His disciples indeed. And we [would] know the truth, and the truth [would] make us free (John 8: 31–32 KJV). Let us always remember that whoever wins the mind wins the body.

Prayer:

Thank You, Jesus, that You have delivered me from every addictive spirit of lust and idol worship. I am made free from every lustful desire and idolatrous thought that is not of You. For on the cross, You paid the price for me to be set free from every greedy longing of the mind, psychological, and physiological trigger. I give You my whole heart, and I thank You for filling every void so that the things of this life do not creep in and take a place that belongs only to You.

Help me, Father of glory, to have the mind of Christ and not one of obsessions. Only You can show me how to have a mind of discipline and self-control. "For you have not given me a spirit of fear, but of power, love, and a sound mind" (2 Timothy 1:7 KJV). I praise my Jesus that I am set free from the power of Satan and his demons that wanted to control my spirit, soul, and body. Jesus, You are the same yesterday, today, and forever. I am asking You now to show me how to operate or be just like You in every way.

Thank You, Lord, for setting me free from any and all addictions. Jesus, You said that You were the light of the world and that, if I followed You, I would not walk in darkness but have the light of life. Thank You, Holy Spirit, for teaching me how to follow Jesus. Help me to see clearly where I am going.

Jesus, You also said that if I continue in Your Word, then I would be Your disciple indeed. I would then know the truth, and the truth would make me free. I choose to hold fast to Your teachings and live in accordance with them, and I thank You, Jesus, that Your truth makes me free from any and all addictions. I'm not trying to get free; I thank You, Lord, for making me free. You set me free from every habit-forming substance, behavior, or activity that has any harmful effects in my actions or deeds.

Glory to God that You have "disarmed every principality and power that was ranged against me" (Colossians 2:15 AMPC). Demons that brought addictive behaviors and thoughts can no longer keep me locked up in death. I have been redeemed from the curse of breaking God's laws. That means You purchased my freedom from what was holding me captive and keeping me in bondage. I am free and liberated from _____ (fill in the blank, such as sexual addictions, bad social interactions, drugs, tremors, anger, hatred, depression, worry, fear, anxiety, food, being judgmental or critical, etc.).

Lord, You said if I called on You in the day of trouble, You would deliver me and honor me. I am calling on You to deliver me from _____ (fill in the blank). Help me not to be misled by the enemy or by people. You said evil communications corrupt good manners, morals, and character. Help me to stay away from things that my heart condemns and what would corrupt my character. Thank You, Jesus, that You set me free from the lust of the flesh, the lust of the eyes, and the pride of life. Because You are my Shepherd, I shall not live in want. I refuse to live in and be controlled by the cravings of the world and my body. For I am fully satisfied by You without withdrawals. Your perfect peace calms every craving, bad appetite, or urge to do wrong.

Thank You, Lord, that no temptation has overtaken me that is not common to mankind. But God, You are faithful, and You will not let me be tempted beyond what I can bear. But when I am tempted, You will also provide me with a way out so that I can endure. Thank You, Jesus, for rescuing me every time I am tempted. Father, You said through every temptation that You would give us a way of escape. I thank You that I see my way of escape in every temptation and I take it every time. I give You praise, glory, and honor for being my miracle-working God and Creator. Thank You that You're the glory and lifter of my head.

I am grateful that I always have a way to escape wrong choices when I look to You. Thank You, Jesus, for setting me free from devils that would try to oppress me in my mind or my thinking. My spirit, soul (mind, will, and emotions), and body belong to You.

I commit those to You today, and I look to renew them daily through Your Word. I wash my mind today through Your words. Let Your words overthrow the lies of every addictive, idolatrous, and obsessive thought coming from the evil one. I cast down every thought exalting itself against the knowledge of Your Word now. I bring every thought into the obedience of Christ today. If Jesus did not teach it, I will not allow it to stay in my mind. I command all oppressive, lustful, and addictive thoughts to go *now* in Jesus's name! Amen.

6

PRAYERS FOR TRANSFORMATION INTO JESUS'S LIKENESS

Genesis 1:26; Daniel 5:12; John 15:2; Romans 8:29; 9:30; 2 Corinthians 3:18; 5:17; Galatians 5:22–24; Ephesians 3:16; Philippians 2:5, 13; 3:21; 1 Peter 1:16; 2 Peter 1:3–7; 1 John 3:1–3

My Notes:

The Merriam-Webster Dictionary defines the word "transformation" as an act, process, or instance of transforming or being transformed. It is the operation of changing (as by rotation or mapping) one configuration or expression into another. You can change or convert by insertion, deletion, or permutation.[22] We should allow God to transform us into the image or likeness of Christ. Jesus needs to insert Himself in our hearts and minds and delete our old man and ways of thinking. He needs to permute, which means to change the order or arrangement of what is in us that does not align with His way of doing and being right by pruning us. John 15:2 says it perfectly. "Any branch in me that does not bear fruit [that stops bearing] He cuts away (trims off, takes away); and He cleanses and repeatedly prunes every branch that continues to bear fruit, to make it bear more and richer and

---

22   *Merriam-Webster*, s.v., "transformation (*n.*)," accessed July 31, 2020, https://www.merriam-webster.com/dictionary/transformation.

more excellent fruit" (AMPC). Not only will the Lord transform us by pruning us, but He can also transform us when we spend time in His presence. As you spend time worshipping Him until His glory comes down and touches you, your spirit, soul, and body will radically change.

The glory of God is His manifested presence when God comes down and physically touches humanity with His power, wisdom, and goodness. The Hebrew word for "glory" is *kavod*.[23] The encyclopedia defines the word *kavod* as heavy, weighty, importance, deference, respect, honor, and majesty. Therefore, a solid biblical definition for glory means to be weighted down or heavy with everything good. I heard this in a sermon from Billye Brim called *The Blood and the Glory* and almost jumped out of my chair with excitement. We need the glory of God to transform us into the likeness of Jesus. We have to have an ability from God to do for us what we cannot do for ourselves. If God does not influence us with His power and ability, we will stay the same and never change.

Prayer:

Thank You, Lord, that we shall be just like You in every area of our lives. Therefore, I purify myself just as You are pure, Lord Jesus. I thank You for all of the pruning, deletions, and permutations that convert me into Your very own image. I praise You, oh Lord, for granting me out of the rich treasury of Your glory to be strengthened and reinforced with mighty power in my inner man by the Holy Spirit. Thank You for indwelling my innermost being and personality. I want to be just like You, Lord Jesus. I behold

---

23 *Strong's Concordance*, Bible hub.com, "3519. Kabowd," accessed March 4, 2020, https://biblehub.com/hebrew/3519.htm.

as in a mirror Your glory. For I am being constantly changed and transformed into Your same image from one degree of glory to the next level of glory by the Spirit of the Lord. As I behold Your way of being and doing right in the Scriptures, I ask You to keep molding me daily into the image of what I am supposed to look like in the Word. Jesus, You are my image, mirror, picture, and reflection of how I should look, act, and respond to life's tests and trials. Thank You, Jesus, for loading me down with everything good from You.

Lord, You said from the beginning, "Let us make man in our image and in our likeness." I want to be just like You in every way. I die to myself to embrace Your life. For we were predestined to be conformed to the image of the Son. Yes, Lord, You are transforming my vile, lowly, natural, and earthly body into a heavenly, glorious body.

I thank You, Lord, that I am holy as You are holy. Thank You, Lord, for working in me to will and to do Your good pleasure. I believe that I am in Christ and I am a new creation. The old things about me have passed away and *all* things about me have become new. Through the power of the Holy Spirit, I am letting the same mind that was in Christ Jesus be in me.

I have the nine attitudes of Jesus working in me by the power of the Holy Spirit. Lord, I thank You that Your precious fruit of the Spirit changes me and gives me the same attitude and mindset that Jesus had while He was on the earth. Father, the work that Your Spirit and presence within me produces is love, joy, peace, longsuffering, gentleness, goodness, faith, meekness, and temperance. Thank You, Holy Spirit, for giving me gladness, patience, an even temper, forbearance, kindness, benevolence, humility, self-control, self-restraint, and freedom from sexual immorality. You make me faithful in all things. Help me not to be lazy or slothful or to procrastinate. Instead, Lord, You have made me diligent, sharp, and quick to respond with a do-it-now mentality.

Thank You, Lord, for giving me an excellent spirit. Because You are no respecter of persons, I thank You, Lord, that, just like Daniel, You give me superior wisdom, knowledge, and understanding to interpret dreams, an ability to clarify riddles, and the power to solve knotty problems.

Father, I am grateful that Your divine power has given unto us all things that pertain to life and godliness. This free gift makes us righteous. Moreover, I know that this righteousness or right standing with you cannot be earned by works, but rather it is imputed or inserted by you. So thank You for allowing me to have this free gift of righteousness based on and produced by faith. I am so blessed that I don't have to try to be good or just like You. I instead receive the free gift that Your divine power has given me. For You have *given* me the knowledge of Jesus, who called me to His glory and virtue. Also, You have *given* me exceeding great and precious promises so that I may be a partaker of Your divine nature by faith.

Because of this, I escape the corruption that is in the world through lust and greed. You also *give* diligence, which adds faith to the virtue you've given me, and to the virtue knowledge, and to knowledge temperance, and to temperance patience, and to patience godliness, and to godliness brotherly kindness, and to brotherly kindness love. Lord, I am so thankful for all the precious things that You have *given* me. I am so grateful that I don't have to earn Your free gifts. Because of Your free gifts, I am never barren or unfruitful.

I thank You also for the spiritual gifts that the Holy Spirit *gives* to us as we obey You. Thank You, Holy Spirit, for the divine grace that is operating in my soul. I have the mind of Christ. I'm letting that same mind that was in Christ Jesus be in me. Because You have *given* me the ability to think like Jesus, I can now act like Jesus at all times. Amen.

7

PRAYERS FOR CONSECRATION

Psalm 51:10; Acts 3:26; Romans 6:13; 12:1–2; 1 Corinthians 6:19–20; 2 Corinthians 8:5; Galatians 2:20; Colossians 3:5–14; 2 Timothy 2:20–21; 1 Peter 1:16; 2:9

My Notes:

The Merriam-Webster Dictionary says the synonyms for the word "consecration" are "blessing," "hallowing," and "sanctification."[24] Therefore, when I think of this word, I see a person coming away by themselves to pray. I imagine that person bowing down before the Father and making a fresh commitment to Him and to Him alone. They may use this time to sanctify and purify themselves or to reaffirm their dedication to the Lord and not to the world or people. This may be a time to cut off the things in their lives that do not belong. This shows God that He is more important than anything else in this world. To do this completely will take a special ability from God. The scriptures say in Acts 3:26 that God "raised up his Son Jesus, sent him to bless you, in turning away every one of you from his iniquities" (KJV). We are blessed when God gives us His grace and we turn away from sin.

---

24 *Merriam-Webster*, s.v., "consecration (*n.*)," accessed July 31, 2020, https://www.merriam-webster.com/dictionary/consecration.

My pastor has often told me that grace is the ability of God's unconditional love, doing for you what you cannot do for yourself. It is God's unmerited favor and blessing. It is divine favor at its best. It is not something that you can earn but rather something that you just receive by faith. You do not deserve it, and it is often unexpected. Grace is love and mercy all wrapped up into one. You cannot live a consecrated life to God without His grace. We all need God's unconditional love, doing for us what we cannot do for ourselves in difficult areas.

Prayer:

Lord Jesus, I bow my knees to Your lordship and admit my dependency on You for all things. You are my Lord and my God, and I will have no other gods or idols before You. You take first place in my heart and mind. Take control of my spirit, soul, and body in Jesus's name. Thank You for sending Jesus to bless me and take all my sins away.

Lord, I commit myself to You. I desire not my will but Your will to be done in my life, on this earth as it is in heaven. I want Your plans, Your purposes, and Your pursuits. Jesus, I cannot do anything in my own strength. Your Word says that I can do all things through You who gives and infuses inner strength into me. Therefore, through Your power, efficiency, and might, I submit myself to Your lordship. Thank You, Lord, for a fresh supply of Your ability and grace to resist evil tendencies. I consecrate and dedicate my life solely to You. It is no longer I that lives, but Christ is living through me and in me.

Lord, I am crucified with Jesus to my feelings and emotions. I am raised with Jesus to a new consecrated and dedicated life set apart wholly unto You. The life I am now living in the flesh is not my own. I am now living by the faith of the Son of God, who loved me and gave Himself for me. Help me, Lord, today to not frustrate the grace of God in my life. I need more of Your grace and Your ability to do for me what I cannot do for myself. Your grace helps me to resist evil temptations and mindsets, for I am only Yours.

Change me, Lord Jesus, into Your very own image. I thank You, Lord, for helping me to escape the corruption in this world through lust and greed. I am an instrument of Your glory and power. Use me, Lord, as a vessel of honor, so that I can be fit for the Master's use. I refuse to be a vessel of dishonor.

Lord, I thank You for teaching me who You made me in Christ Jesus. Thank You that my body is the temple of the Holy Ghost, and I choose to glorify God in my body. I have been bought with a price. You paid for my body through the precious blood of Jesus. Thank You, Lord, for the blood of Jesus that washes me and cleanses me from all unrighteousness. Lord, I dedicate myself to You today. I ask You to make me holy as You are holy by sanctifying, hallowing, and purifying me in the blood of Jesus. Father of Glory, as I become the vessel of honor fit for the Master's use because of Your sanctification, I thank You for taking my life and doing something good with it. In Jesus's name. Amen.

8

PRAYERS FOR AUTHORITY

Isaiah 54:17; Matthew 28:18; Mark 1:27; 3:14–15; 11:22–26; Luke 10:19; John 14:14; 15:7; Acts 5:32; Romans 8:37; 13:1; 1 Corinthians 12:8–10; Ephesians 1:17–21; Colossians 2:15; Titus 3:1;

Hebrews 13:17; James 4:7

My Notes:

The Merriam-Webster Dictionary describes authority as: "1. The power to give orders or make decisions: the power or right to direct or control someone or something. 2. The confident quality of someone who knows a lot about something or who is respected or obeyed by other people. 3. A quality that makes something seem true or real."[25]

Jesus is the true definition of authority, and He gave us His authority to use against the forces of darkness. Jesus said in Luke 10:19, "Behold! I have given you authority and power to trample upon serpents and scorpions, and [physical and mental strength and ability] over all the power that the enemy [possesses]; and nothing shall in any way harm you" (AMPC). The Father in heaven gave Jesus the right to give orders, make decisions, and

---

25   *Merriam-Webster*, s.v., "authority (*n.*)," accessed March 4, 2020, https://www.merriam-webster.com/dictionary/authority.

direct and control devils. He knew a lot about God and how to use His power. By doing this, Jesus was so respected that even people who did not like Him had to obey Him. Jesus's power was real, true, and felt by all who came in contact with Him.

True authority and power only come when we recognize the power that is found in Jesus's name. However, Jesus's name is not just His name. You don't know a person from just knowing that person's name. To really know them, you must spend time with them and get to know them intimately. Generally, you really understand who a person is by the words that they speak. Therefore, when we talk about Jesus's name, we are talking about His love, power, character, and authority. So when you see Jesus teaching in John 14:14, "If ye shall ask anything in [His] name, [He] will do it," you will realize that means whatever you ask in His love, power, character or authority, He will do (AMPC). When you spend time in Jesus's words and get to know Him, you begin to see what He has given you to defeat the works of Satan and his demons. One of the names of God is Jehovah Sabaoth, which means the God of angel armies. He is the Lord of hosts or armies, and they are at our disposal whenever we need them.

Prayer:

Lord, thank You for my seat of authority that You have given me in the heavenlies by Your side. Thank You, Lord, that I am seated with Christ on His throne over all the works of darkness and nothing shall by any means hurt me. Thank You, Father of Glory, that You have seated me above every principality, power, might, and dominion that is named in this earth. I take my place of authority beside Christ to bind every evil spirit, ruler of the darkness of this world, and spiritual wickedness in high places.

I bind their operation in my family, church, and government in Jesus's name. No weapon formed against us shall prosper. I command these evil spirits to take their hands off my family, money, spirit, soul, and body in Jesus's name.

I thank You, Lord, that You have given me authority and power over all the power the enemy possesses and nothing shall by any means hurt me. Jesus, I believe that You have disarmed every principality and power that could ever be ranged against me in Jesus's name. I believe You made a show of them openly and triumphed over them through what You did for me on the cross. I have exceeding greatness of power over all demons in all their forms and manifestations.

Thank You, Jesus, that the Father gave You *all* power in heaven and on earth. I am grateful that You, in turn, show that power to us. Because of the power that You have given me, I can stop all of the attacks, delays, strategies, advances, schemes, and devices of the wicked one.

Lord, I recognize the authority that You set up in the earth, and I bow my knees to Your lordship. Your Word says that if we submit to You, we are able to resist the devil, and he has to flee from us. Father, I cannot see You, but I can see who You established to rule on the earth. Therefore, I submit to my spiritual leader(s), my spouse, and my supervisors by recognizing the authority they have been given in their roles. I know, Lord, that they keep watch over my soul and help to guard my spiritual welfare. Help us, Lord, not to mumble, grumble, or complain at their instructions. I thank You, Lord, that, because I have bowed down to the order that you ordained from the foundation of the world, I am now able to resist all of the enemy's plots and plans for my life.

Thank You, Jesus, that You gave me the power to command unclean spirits and they obey me in Your name. You also appointed me to continue with You in preaching and teaching people about Your love, power, character, and authority. Thank You for giving me the power and authority to heal the sick and drive out demons.

Father, I am grateful that You have given me the right to ask whatsoever I will in Jesus's name. Jesus said that He would do it if I abide in Him and His words abide in me. I am abiding in Jesus. Therefore, I now get to ask what I will and see You do it. Glory to God for this kind of power and for the free gift that has been given to me.

Your Word also says that if I speak to the mountains or the seemingly impossible things in my life and tell them to be removed and cast into the sea without doubt in my heart, they will obey me. I refuse to doubt your ability. I speak to whatever doesn't belong in my life, and I command all of it to be removed in Jesus's name. Because of the authority You have given me, it has to obey me. For You said that You give Your precious Holy Spirit to those who obey You. I obey You, Lord. Therefore, I get to resist the enemy and watch him run from me in terror. Go now, doubt, confusion, unbelief, poverty, lack, rebellion, worry, fear, deception, sickness, disease, stress, lies, anger, hatred, racism, bias, and lust in Jesus's name. Lord, I know that You are great in all the earth. You're bigger than anything I could ever face or imagine.

Father, the more I yield to Your divine grace, the more I will see Your endowments, gifts, and extraordinary powers that distinguish me as a Christian. Thank You, Holy Spirit, for manifesting Your power through me to speak messages of wisdom; express words of knowledge and understanding; and operate in wonder-working faith, extraordinary powers of healing, working of miracles, prophetic insights, and gifts to interpret God's divine will and purpose. You also give me the ability to discern between true spirits and false ones, along with speaking various kinds of tongues and an ability to interpret those tongues. Thank You that You empower me to win and conquer the impossible things in this life.

The power of Your love also protects me as well. Thank You, Lord, for leading, guiding, and helping me not to sadden or vex the Holy Spirit by speaking foolishness. For, Jesus would only speak what the Father told Him to say. Help me not to disregard the teachings of Christ but to put them into practice in my everyday life. His words are the authority and the power of almighty God.

Holy Spirit, bring revelation from heaven concerning the Scriptures. Make them come alive and explain them to me in a way that I may walk and live in them every day. Lord, show me how You made me more than a conqueror and not the devil's victim. Keep showing me what it means to be a conqueror. Thank You for what You've given me on this earth so that I can use it to declare Your name boldly in Jesus's name.

Thank You for the power and authority You've given us as Christians on this earth to fight off the plots and schemes of the enemy. Thank You for bringing those plans to nothing so that they are of no effect in my life. I thank You that You have disarmed the principalities and powers that were ranged against my life and that no weapon formed against me shall prosper.

Thank You, Jehovah Sabaoth, for Your hosts of angels and the ministering spirits that You have encamped about us with shouts of deliverance. They are ministering on my behalf right now by fighting for me and protecting me. You are the God of angel armies, and I thank You for going to war on our behalf. Amen.

9

PRAYERS FOR FORGIVENESS

Matthew 5:44; Mark 11:25–26; Luke 23:34; John 13:34; Romans 5:5, 8; 1 Corinthians 10:13; Ephesians 3:16–20; 4:32; 1 John 1:9; 2:16; Jude 1:24

My Notes:

Jesus gave us a new commandment to love one another as He loved us on the cross. This is found in John 13:34. The question is, "How did Jesus love us?" To see how Jesus loved us, we need to look at Romans 5:8. Christ loved us while we were yet sinners. He did not make us earn or deserve His love. His love will love you before you ever do anything right and while you have everything wrong. His love provides the way for us to love like Him and come out of darkness. If you do not see how God loved you first through Jesus while you were guilty, you will never understand how to love others the way Jesus said to love them. The new commandment tells you to love yourself first with Jesus's love and then give that love away to another. Without receiving and giving the love of Jesus to yourself first, you can never give that love to someone else. It is hard to give away what you do not have.

Never fear that you do not have the love of God in you if you are a Christian. Romans 5:5 says that the love of God was shed abroad in our hearts by the Holy Spirit. That means that He poured the same kind of love that God is into our hearts. This happened when we asked Jesus to come into our hearts and save us. Therefore, God gave us the ability to love people with the same love and the same capacity that He is.

Prayer:

Father of glory, I renounce the spirit of unforgiveness in Jesus's name. I forgive everyone who has ever done me wrong. I release them from my heart and mind. Lord, I love them, You love them, and we love them. I release them, and I will not remember any negativity, bad situations, or circumstances. I also release all negative and toxic emotions in Jesus's name. Lord, erase the stain, sting, and guilt of whatever was done wrong to me in Jesus's name. Lord, teach us how to love like You, walk like You, and talk like You. Your Word says that I have the same capability to love people even as You love them. So I love them with joy, just like You loved me, even those who do not like me.

Lord, I belong to You, and I choose to give people what You have freely given me. I will not make anyone earn or deserve my love in Jesus's name. They do not have to live good enough to get me to like them. For your love cannot be earned.

Lord, when I stand praying, I forgive if I have any ought (anything big or small) against anyone. I forgive whether or not their actions were intentional. I forgive at all times because I always want You to forgive me. Therefore, I will not harbor unforgiveness toward others. Your Word says if I don't forgive others, then You won't forgive me. I want to be forgiven, so I choose to forgive. I forgive everyone in my past and present and those who may do me wrong in the future.

(You cannot have any unforgiveness against people, places, or things, especially yourself. If you hold onto unforgiveness, you will cease your growth in the Father's love. That means you must let go of every icky or sticky situation that may arise. If you hold on to grudges, harbor anger, or any resentment in your heart, God cannot forgive you when you ask.)

Thank You, Father, that this love has been shed abroad in my heart by the Holy Spirit. You have given me Your power and ability to forgive others the way You forgave me. Help me not to make people earn or deserve my forgiveness based on their performance and what they do, right or wrong. But, let me forgive based on my faith in what You did for me on the cross.

Yes, Lord, You poured Your very self into me so that I can love just as You do. You have given me Your power and ability to forgive others the way You forgave me.

I choose to remember John 13:34, where You have given me a commandment to love others the way You have loved me. I see that You have loved me and others while we were yet sinners. Because I see this example in You, and You are in me, I choose to love others while they are yet sinners. I do not make people earn my love or forgiveness. Lord, help me to love people even if I do not receive their love back in return. It is more important for me to love them than it is for them to love me.

Lord, I give this gift of love away freely and graciously. As freely as I have received it, I give it away to others. Lord, as You help me, I will love, bless, and do good to those who despitefully use and persecute me. I will pray the same prayer in the same way that Jesus prayed on the cross. I will say, Father, forgive them for they know not what they do. Have mercy on my enemies. Help them to come to the knowledge of the truth that is in Christ Jesus. I declare that I am free from all bitterness, anger, strife, hatred, jealousy, envy, malice, and rage in Jesus's name.

(Malice is an evil habit of the mind. When people operate in malice, they have ill will toward others. This comes with an intention or desire to do evil to someone, according to the dictionary.)[26]

Lord, help me to grow in love and forgiveness daily. I want to know the depth, length, and height of this love. Help me to be wholly filled and flooded with You, Lord God. I want the richest fullness of Your divine presence that I can possibly have. I thank You that my body is wholly filled and flooded with Your love and not hatred or strife. Lord, as I stay full of Your love, You began to do super-abundantly far over and above all that I dare ask or think. Because I choose to forgive, You go beyond my highest prayers, desires, thoughts, hopes, or dreams in answering those prayers.

I thank you, Master Jesus, for the privilege and honor I have to confess my sins. You said that You are faithful and just to forgive us and cleanse us from all unrighteousness. Therefore, I confess the sin of _____ (fill in the blank), and I thank You for forgiving me and cleansing me of that forever.

Lord Jesus, I am not only asking that You forgive me for all my wrongdoings, but I am asking You to teach me how to walk free from all sin. Teach me how not to give in to the temptations of the

26   *Merriam-Webster*, s.v., "malice (*n.*)," accessed March 4, 2020, https://www.merriam-webster.com/dictionary/malice.

devil and the flesh. You are able to keep me from stumbling and falling. You are able to show me a way of escape whenever I am tempted. Help me take my way of escape every time. Don't let me yield to the dictates of the flesh but rather to the Holy Spirit's promptings. Thank You, Jesus, for keeping me free from the lust of the flesh, the lust of the eyes, and the pride of life.

Thank You, Lord, for Your forgiveness and for how You loved me while I was yet a sinner. The love You showed me while I was messed up helped me to come out of some grave mistakes, shame, guilt, hurts, dangers, and pains from my past. I choose to let go of my past failures and mistakes forever.

I see the weaknesses in my flesh, but it is not to bring condemnation or guilt but rather to bring me light and hope. Thank You for washing me in the blood from my past, and I pray that my past does not negatively affect my future. Father, I pray that the Holy Spirit will give me wisdom and understanding to correct what I have allowed before I really knew You, served You, or understood Your love. Amen.

10

PRAYERS FOR HEALING

Deuteronomy 7:15, 28; 30:19; Psalm 30:2; 91:10; 103:1–5; 107:20; Proverbs 18:21; Isaiah 53:4–5; 58:8; Matthew 6:10; 8:17; 12:25; 18:18–20; Mark 11:22–25; Luke 10:19; John 14:6, 14, 27; 15:7; Acts 10:38; Romans 5:17; 8:2; Galatians 3:13; Colossians 2:15; Hebrews 11:1, 6; 1 Peter 2:24; 1 John 3:22; 3 John 1:2

My Notes:

The power of God that comes to us through Jesus has the power to raise our natural bodies to a heavenly state of being and dignity. A born-again child of God has the right to walk in divine health. It is not just a nice idea to be sickness and disease free. We become citizens of heaven when we give our lives to Christ. No one is sick in heaven, and Jesus told the disciples in Matthew 6:10 they could have on earth as it is in heaven. If no one in heaven is sick, then I don't have to be sick on the earth.

Knowing these spiritual truths causes you to fight in a different way when something attacks your body. I must learn how to take the name of Jesus and make the devil stop. We have the right to tell Satan and his demons to take their hands off our bodies in Jesus's name. We also get to tell sicknesses, diseases, spirits of infirmity, and anything else that does not belong in our bodies to be removed from us and cast into the sea. Sicknesses and diseases were disarmed like all the other works of the enemy by Jesus on the cross over two thousand years ago. He actually nailed them to His cross. He then gave us His power and authority over *all* the power the enemy possesses in Luke 10:19. He also taught us that nothing shall by any means hurt us.

This is because Jesus gave us His power and ability—not ours—to defeat the works of darkness. He taught us what to speak against their works when they show up in Mark 11: 23–24. Jesus said, "For verily I say unto you, That whosoever shall say unto this mountain, Be thou removed, and be thou cast into the sea; and shall not doubt in his heart, but shall believe that those things which he saith shall come to pass; he shall have whatsoever he saith. Therefore, I say unto you, What things soever ye desire, when ye pray, believe that you receive them, and ye shall have them" (KJV). From these verses, we see that we should do three times more speaking than believing. Furthermore, the speaking should be done directly to the mountain or, in this case, the illness or infirmity. We must speak to the physical or mental symptoms and tell them to be removed from our body. This is more than just praying for healing. This is using Jesus's power that He has already given you when you accepted Him.

We begin to use and activate this power only through words. We must speak the promises of God from the Word and not the problem, because life and death are in the power of the tongue. (See Proverbs 18:21.) When you understand the power of words, you will see that by speaking the promises of God, you are actually choosing life. In Deuteronomy 30:19, God says, "I call heaven and earth to record this day against you, [that] I have set before you life and death, blessing and cursing: therefore choose life, that both thou and thy seed may live" (KJV).

Romans 5:17 discusses the fact that because of one man's sin (Adam), death reigned upon all men. Adam's rebellion opened the door for Satan to reign in this life with his kingdom of death and destruction instead of God and man. This brought curses of sickness, disease, poverty, lack, and separation from God's blessed influence upon man. This curse affects everyone—babies, teenagers, the elderly—everyone. It was truly upon all men. However, because of one man's obedience or sacrifice for sins (Jesus), life and man began to reign again and have dominion over everything that God had created. From this explanation, we can dispel the myth that God puts sicknesses and diseases on people to teach them lessons. God cannot do both the healing and the killing. Jesus taught that "every kingdom divided against itself is brought to desolation; and every city or house divided against itself shall not stand" (Matthew 12:25 KJV).

Assuredly, Galatians 3:13 tells us that Jesus has redeemed us from the curse of breaking God's laws. This means that Jesus took the punishment that you and I deserve for what we did wrong on Himself when he died on the cross. "Redeemed" means He purchased our freedom from all curses, no matter the form or manifestation. Also, take notice that the word "has" is past tense. This implies that whatever you are bringing to God as it relates to healing is a finished work. In addition, Jesus said in 1 Peter 2:24 that with the stripes that wounded Him, we were healed and made whole. If I *were* healed, then I *am* healed right now. Don't lose sight of the fact that faith is now and not later. Again, we have another finished work. For faith pulls the finished work of Christ to my present condition, reality, state, or circumstance. These are very important truths as they relate to healing.

All symptoms that are manifesting in your body are facts and lies, but they are not the truth that is in Christ Jesus. Remember to see life through Jesus's reality and not from the doctor's facts or the enemy's lies and false symptoms. Once you believe, you receive your healing and take it by faith. All symptoms trying to manifest again are to be returned to the sender, Satan. My friend Jan, who was supernaturally healed of blown out discs in her neck, told me this. Later, lying symptoms came back and told her she was not healed. The Lord then gave her a dream of a package being delivered to her door. She opened the door, and it was her symptoms. The Lord told her not to take the package but to return it to the sender. This is where you demand Satan and his demons to go and tell him not to come back. I tell sickness and disease, "I will not receive your lies, so take your hands off my body in Jesus's name. Go lie to someone else who does not know who they are in Christ. Go tell your lies to someone who does not know the power Jesus has given them, because I refuse to put up with this bondage in Jesus's name." Glory to God, Jesus came to set the captive free.

In a sermon on healing, Norvel Hayes taught people to make all sicknesses and diseases eat Matthew, Mark, Luke, and John for breakfast, lunch, and dinner. If you put enough faith pressure on any illness, it will flee from your body. The enemy cannot handle the Word of God or a person who is locked in on those promises without wavering because of facts or symptoms. According to Acts 10:38, sicknesses and diseases are satanic oppressions. Jesus was anointed by God to go around and do good by healing all who were oppressed of the devil, for God was with Him.

Again, note that being healed is not just a nice idea but a divine right for every born-again child of God. Jesus paid a price on the cross for our healing when He was beaten for our guilt and iniquities. We must demand and enforce our rights, or Satan will steal them from us just like he did to Adam.

Prayer:

I thank You, Lord, that with the stripes that wounded Jesus, I was healed and made whole of every sickness, disease, pain, and torment in Jesus's name. If I was healed on the cross when You took stripes on Your back, then I am healed today. Therefore, body, line up with the Word of God and be made whole in Jesus's name. I speak to _____ (name the pain, fever, sickness, or disease) and command it to be removed and cast into the midst of the sea in Jesus's name. I command this sickness to dry up, die, wither, and disappear in Jesus's name. Sickness/disease/spirit of infirmity, you can't stay in my body. I command you to go in the name of Jesus. I speak the life of Christ to my body.

Thank You, Lord, that the same power that raised Jesus from the dead is working in my body to raise it to a heavenly state of being and dignity. I speak health and life to my spirit, soul, and body. Thank You, Lord, for the angels repairing any form of destruction and death in my body right now. I bind the spirit of death in Jesus's name. I will live and not die and declare the works of the Lord.

Lord, I give You glory, honor, and praise that my body functions in divine health. Every working part functions in the proper order and alignment the way it was designed to function in heaven. I speak health and life to my whole flesh from the top of my head to the soles of my feet.

Thank You, Jesus, that God anointed You with the Holy Ghost and with power, and You went about doing good and healing all who were oppressed of the devil. I'm so happy that You live in me, and I am anointed with the same Holy Ghost empowerment just like You. Satan, take your hands off my body in Jesus's name. I don't belong in your family, and I am not in your kingdom. I have been translated from the kingdom of darkness into the kingdom of the Son of the Father's love. It is my divine right to walk in divine health.

Thank You, Jesus, for bearing our grief and carrying away our sorrows. Thank You for being wounded for my transgressions and being bruised for my iniquities. You took the needed chastisement for us to obtain peace, and because of that, we are healed and made whole. Because of You, Jesus, my health is springing forth speedily. Glory to God, You took my infirmities and bore all my sicknesses and diseases. I do not consider my physical senses, including the doctor's words or any symptoms in my body, but I meditate on the words from Jesus's lips.

Thank You, Jesus, that the Spirit of life that is in You has freed me from the law of sin and death. Lord, I know that sin and sickness are twins, but I thank You that You have set me free from their curses forever. For I cried unto You, and You healed me. Therefore, no evil shall befall me and neither can any plague come nigh my dwelling. Thank You, Jesus, that You have healed all my diseases, and You have redeemed my life from destruction. Thank You for sending Your Word and healing me today.

Thank You, Jesus, that You have redeemed us from the curse of breaking God's laws as You promised in Deuteronomy 28. We are free from the curse of sickness and disease, poverty, lack, and separation from God's blessed influence that came when the people of God did not obey Him. Lord, I'm so thankful that Christ purchased our freedom from all of these curses when He died for us on the cross.

Thank You, Lord, that I prosper and walk in divine health even as my soul prospers and is in health. Jesus, You said that whatever I ask for in Your name, You would do it. I ask that I be completely healed and made whole in Jesus's name. Thank You, Lord, for perfect peace.

Thank You, Jesus, that Your name equals Your love, power, character, and authority. Thank you for Your peace, which means to be whole, complete, entire, and lacking or wanting nothing.[27] When I am in perfect peace, nothing is broken or missing in my life spiritually, physically, emotionally, mentally, financially, socially, and intellectually. Jesus said He was the Prince of Peace. Glory to God!

Because of Your perfect peace, I will not allow myself to be agitated or disturbed based on what circumstances look or feel like in Jesus's name. I speak peace over my spirit, soul, and body in Jesus's name. Lord, I refuse to be afraid of any negative reports or facts from doctors. They are not the truth that is in Christ Jesus. Jesus's truth says that with the stripes that wounded Him, I was, am, and will be made whole forever.

---

27   *Strong's Concordance*, Bible hub.com, "7965. Shalom," accessed March 4, 2020, https://biblehub.com/hebrew/7965.htm.

Jesus, Your Word says that whatever we ask, we receive of You because we keep Your commandments and do those things that are pleasing in Your sight. Lord, I obey You and do what You say; therefore, I get to ask that no sicknesses, diseases, pains, torments, or anything else that wants to harass me can stay in my body in the name of Jesus.

I believe that I am healed today, according to the Word! Amen.

11

PRAYERS FOR FAMILY

Psalm 112:1–2; Isaiah 54:17; Matthew 18:19–20; Luke 6:46–49; John 10:4–5; 13:34; Romans 4:20; 12:2 (TPT), 12:21; 1 Corinthians 10:13; 13:4–8; Galatians 5:16–22; Ephesians 5:21; 6:1,10,12; 2 Timothy 2:3–5, 26; Hebrews 1:14; James 3:16; 4:7; 1 Peter 3:9–10; 1 John 3:8

My Notes:

Satan hates the family because when people are in unity, they can destroy his kingdom through their agreement. Jesus said in Matthew 18:19–20, "Again I say unto you, That if two of you shall agree on earth as touching anything that they shall ask, it shall be done for them of my Father which is in heaven. For where two or three are gathered together in my name, there am I in the midst of them." We can see Jesus manifest if we are in harmony with one another.

Contrastingly, James 3:16 explains that, "For where envying and strife is, there is confusion and every evil work" (KJV). Satan wants to make even close family members envious and jealous of one another. His goal is to divide and conquer so that he can rule and control the environment or home. If he can keep you mad, angry, and upset, you will not be submitted to God who is love. Then, if you are not submitted to love, he does not have to flee your home. Check out James 4:7 which says, "Submit yourselves therefore to God. Resist the devil, and he will flee from you" (KJV). If you are praying and nothing is happening or the situation becomes worse, check your heart for submission or strife.

This is why it is vital to fight and maintain the unity, harmony, love, joy, and peace in your family at all costs. But you can only do this by learning to fight in the Spirit. Ephesians 6:12 says, "We wrestle not against flesh and blood, but against principalities, against powers, against the rulers of the darkness of this world, against spiritual wickedness in high places" (KJV). To do this practically, we bind up demons bringing strife, hatred, failure, immaturity, lusts, attitudes, moods, fussing, cursing, and fighting in Jesus's name. Tell them to get out of your home in Jesus's name. Invite the Holy Spirit to help and teach you all how to fulfill your roles with joy. "A soft answer turns away wrath, but grievous words stir up anger" (Proverbs 15:1 AMPC). Learn to praise and worship the Father in the beauty of His holiness instead of sulking in silence or responding in rage. Let God satisfy you in every way and don't expect a family member to fill a void that only God can fill.

Ephesians 6:13 indicates that the only way to defeat the attacks of the enemy is to put on the whole armor of God. God is love, so we are putting on the armor of love. This armor helps us to stand in the evil days that we face on this earth.

Prayer:

Thank You, Lord, that no weapon formed against me or my family shall prosper. For You have ordained the family to be a symbol of Your love, unity, and power in Jesus's name. Thank You, Lord, that my children are much smarter than the devil's children. Thank You, Lord, that they are smarter because they hear Your voice and are responsive to the Holy Spirit.

Bless us with wisdom and knowledge to make the right decisions. Let us hear Your voice today, Jesus, and the voices of demons and devils, we will not follow. I plead the blood of Jesus over my family in Jesus's name, and I thank You for the angels that You have sent to be encamped around us. Thank You, Lord, for the ministering spirits sent to minister to us daily because we are joint heirs of Your salvation.

Precious Jesus, who is our example, help us not to live in our feelings and emotions. Show my family that You are greater in tough moments. Teach us how to love each other the way You loved us on the cross because we are better together. Therefore, we need You, Jesus, to give us all the mind of Christ when circumstances seem crazy. Help us not to be envious or jealous of one another. Strengthen us in our inner man by the Holy Ghost when we feel weak in our human flesh. Let us be renewed in the spirit of our minds. Make us intentional about spending time together in the Word of God to wash out old ways of thinking.

Jesus, help my family to see who You made us in Christ and the power that You have given us. Transform us from being the devil's victims to being more than conquerors. Help us not to imitate the ideals and opinions of the culture around us. But, inwardly transform us by the Holy Spirit who reforms the way we think. You are training my family to be strong in faith and to give glory to God.

Lord, show me how to be a godly mother, and show my husband how to be a godly father. Help my husband lead our family with wisdom and integrity. Keep us from perverse men and women who want to distort the truth of God's Word in our lives.. Teach us as parents how to set the right examples for our children to follow us as we follow Christ. Lord, help us not to provoke our children to anger but to raise them in the fear and admonition of the Lord. Give my children the mind of Christ.

Thank you, Holy Spirit, for showing us how to love and submit to one another out of our reverence for Christ. As we practice disciplining ourselves, show us how to keep our tongues free from evil, guile, treachery, and deceit. Then we will see good days and enjoy life with one another. Empower us to never return evil for evil or insult for insult. We do not want to live in strife, scolding, tongue lashings, or berating but rather in blessings. We pray for one another's welfare, happiness, and protection. Give us words to believe and speak to each other in difficult times of tests and trials.

Thank You, Jesus, for teaching us in Luke 6 to come to You, hear what You say, and then do it. We will then have a solid foundation in life. We don't need to only hear Your teachings, but we need to believe and speak them too. If we do this, You said the gates of hell would not prevail against us. However, if we do not come to You, hear Your teachings, or do them, our foundation will be like sand. Then the floods or the tests and trials of life will beat upon our house or life and we will have a great fall. The fall will be great because the foundation of Christ's teachings is the only thing that can make you strong in life. Thank You that we can come to You for everything.

We choose to hear what Jesus teaches us in the Word. We will believe and speak His words and then put them into practice. We will not be hypocrites, fakes, or phonies. Instead, we are vessels of honor fit for the Master's use. Lord, help us to be ambassadors of Christ and to represent Him well to the masses. Don't let Satan teach us and make us a vessel of dishonor, but loose, dissolve, and destroy the works Satan has done or is trying to do to us today.

I thank You, Lord, that my family will not fall today due to temptations. We will forever discern your will and live a beautiful life that is satisfying and perfect in your eyes. Help us to remember what Jesus taught us in the Scriptures. Aid us in coming to our senses to use Jesus's words as a weapon against our enemy. Give us the power to resist and escape the snare of the devil. Help us not to give in to the dictates of the flesh and the perverseness of our soul. But as a family, we choose to renew our minds and overcome evil with good.

Lord, help my family to walk and live habitually in the Holy Spirit. Help us to be responsive to, controlled by, and guided by the Spirit so that we will not gratify the cravings of the flesh. Lord, teach us as a family to operate in the fruit of the Spirit. Then we will have love, joy, peace, longsuffering, gentleness, goodness, faith, meekness, and temperance towards one another.

Lord, teach us as a family to love as You loved us on the cross. Help us to see that Your love never fails. Show us how to daily defeat strife, hatred, malice, and unforgiveness. Help us to keep the unity of the faith, love, and peace at all times. Cover us with the whole armor of God. Your armor of love helps us quench all the fiery darts of the wicked one. Because of who You made us,

Jesus, we are now strong soldiers in your army. With Your love and power, we can endure all challenges like champions.

Thank You, Father, that as my family fears You in reverence and respect and delights greatly in Your commandments, my seed will be mighty upon the earth. You said the generation of the upright shall be blessed. I thank You, Lord, that my children are blessed and mighty on this earth. Amen.

12

PRAYERS FOR WALKING IN LOVE

Matthew 25:40 (NIV); Luke 23:34; John 13:34; 15:12; Romans 5:5, 8; 1 Corinthians 10:3–5; 13:4–8; 14:1 (AMPC); 2 Corinthians 10:3–5 (AMPC); Ephesians 3:16–21; 4:32; 5:1–2; Philippians 1:9–10; 2:5; 4:6–8; 1 John 4:7–12

My Notes:

Living in love is one of the most important areas in our lives to protect because that is who God is. We must grasp the fact that love is not a feeling. It is not the goose bumps you feel when someone you think you love enters the room. God alone is love, apart from any feelings or emotions we may experience. Saying that God is love does not automatically mean that you can just say that love is God. We need a picture of what love looks like, says, and does. We see that picture in Christ. Christ is the visible image of the invisible God. When we see what Jesus did for us on the cross, we can see the best picture of love ever displayed.

The website www.explorerbiblestudy.org informs us that "the Greek language has several words translated by our single word love: *philos* in the Greek is brotherly love; *eros* is sexual love; *agape* is God's love demonstrated in Jesus's sacrifice for the sins of the world at Calvary. Jesus embodied agape—sacrificial love seeking the highest good of another, not an emotion (like affection) but a decision from a deliberate act of the will. The King James Version translates agape as charity, which is love in action."[28] Are you being intentional about walking in love today? Remember, you cannot make people earn or deserve your love. It is a free gift!

Any unforgiveness toward people, places, or things will hinder your growth and keep you from knowing God's love more. It will also keep you from seeing answers to your prayers, as we saw earlier in the book in Ephesians 3:16–21 (AMPC). We must make the decision to walk in love and specifically focus on the thoughts that come into our minds. Second Corinthians 10:3–5 declares, "For though we walk (live) in the flesh, we are not carrying on our warfare according to the flesh and using mere human weapons. For the weapons of our warfare are not physical [weapons of flesh and blood], but they are mighty before God for the overthrow and destruction of strongholds, [Inasmuch as we] refute arguments and theories and reasonings and every proud and lofty thing that sets itself up against the [true] knowledge of God; and we lead every thought and purpose away captive into the obedience of Christ (the Messiah, the Anointed One" (AMPC).

Our fight will never be against people, and strongholds are areas of our minds that are controlled by something other than God's love. These strongholds can manifest in many forms like arguments, strife, etc. So we must be aware of negative thoughts about others and remove them from our minds. We can do this practically by renewing our minds by meditating on love verses and actually speaking to the bad thoughts and telling them to be

---

28   Marni Shideler McKenzie, *The Explorer's Bible Study: 1 Corinthians*, www. explorerbiblestudy.org (Dickson, TN: date unknown) .

removed from our mind. Romans 12:2 tells us to be transformed by the renewing of our minds. If your mind is not washed and cleansed by the washing of the water of the Word, then you will develop malice.

Malice is an evil habit of the mind. Your mind can form a habit of thinking the wrong way. A wrong way of thinking is actually a mindset that thinks the opposite of Jesus's teachings. It is completely against what Jesus taught, said, and did for us on the cross. This mind does not bring every thought into the obedience of Christ. This mindset is not renewed or washed with the pure water of the Word of God. Therefore, it can also be called a diseased soul, which means this mind is truly sick. It is vitally important that we renew our minds or wash out our thinking with the Word of God. Reading the Bible helps us to get rid of our yucky thoughts and puts fresh new thoughts about the impossible into our minds. This is one of the only ways to truly walk in love. We have to be ready to resist evil thoughts about people and situations, knowing the real enemy is Satan and not mankind.

Here is a testimony from my pastor, Pastor Scales. He kept asking Jesus to teach him how to love like Him and to love Him more. Throughout the years, he would pray this prayer over and over. One day, he became a little angry at the Lord and said, "Lord, I have been asking You for years to teach me how to love like You. Why haven't you answered my prayer?"

My pastor said God asked him a question. "How are you loving your wife?" My pastor spoke up with great excitement and joy because he no longer was fussing and fighting with her after two years of arguing together. The Lord had taught him how to be quiet, let her argue by herself, and then bless her, along with their son. He did this while she was still messed up and never gave her what she deserved. The Lord said that because he was loving his wife more, he was really loving Him more.

My pastor had the revelation of what Jesus taught the disciples in Matthew 25:40. Jesus told them, "The King will reply, Truly I tell you, whatever you did for one of the least of these brothers and sisters of mine, you did for me" (NIV). Jesus told them in some verses later that they did not look after Him because they did not help the sick, visit people who were in prison, or clothe the poor. How we treat others matters to Jesus.

Prayer:

Thank You, Lord, for today and for the revelation of Your love. Thank You for the new commandment to love others the way You have loved me. In Romans 5:8, You loved me while I was yet a sinner. You did not make me earn or deserve this love. It was freely given. Therefore, I will love others in the same way that You have loved me on the cross. I will not make others deserve or earn my love. I freely give as I have freely received. Jesus, just like You prayed to the Father, "Forgive them for they know not what they do," I will say and do the same.

Now, Lord Jesus, I need You to help me love others like You, walk like You, and talk like You. I forgive everybody that has ever done me wrong. I loose them. I love them, You love them, and we love them. Continue teaching me how to love people the way You loved them. For You laid down your life for us while we were yet sinners. Help me, Jesus, to see people the way You see them. Give me a heart of compassion and not a heart of stone. I pray that Your love in me may abound yet more and more in all knowledge and judgment. Help me to approve what is excellent and to be sincere and without offense till the day of Christ. Change me, Lord Jesus, into Your image of love.

God, You told me to be an imitator of You, and the Bible says that You are love. I thank You that I am being constantly changed into Your image of love. I know that all thoughts that are not generating from Your love are toxic to me. Therefore, I release all negative energy, emotions, thoughts, and feelings. I refuse to harbor unforgiveness and malice. Help me, Lord, not to be mean or hold grudges toward people, places, or things.

Help me to have the mind of Christ and to cast down every thought and imagination that exalts itself against the knowledge of how much You love me and other people. Train me to think and meditate on Your love at all times. For I want to operate in Your agape love and not a false love that fades based on the circumstances and experiences of life. Your love never fails, fades out, or comes to an end. Change me, Lord, so that I never come to an end with people or give up on them because of their behavior. Lord, you are excellent in all the earth, and You never gave up on me because of my mistakes. Instead, You forgave me before I asked, which is why I can be free now. Thank You, Lord, that I can forgive others before they ask and love them when they have just done the worst thing possible.

Lord, You have empowered me to be an imitator of You and to copy Your example. Thank You, Lord, for helping me to continue to follow You and walk in love, as Christ also has loved me. Jesus, You have given Yourself for me as an offering and sacrifice to the Father because You loved me. Thank You, Lord, that I walk in love and give myself as an offering and sacrifice which is a sweet-smelling savor unto You.

(When you read the love verses in 1 Corinthians 13, you see the attributes of love. You then understand how you should act and respond in life's tests and trials. Put your name in 1 Corinthians 13:4–8 in the Amplified Bible and pray these verses over yourself.)

Lord, Your Word says that love (Erica) endures long and is patient and kind; love (Erica) never is envious nor boils over with jealousy, love (Erica) is not boastful or vainglorious, love (Erica) does not display him/herself haughtily. Love (Erica) is not conceited (arrogant and inflated with pride); love (Erica) is not rude (unmannerly) and does not act unbecomingly. Love (God's love in us) (Erica) does not insist on its own rights or its own way, for it (Erica) is not self-seeking. It (Erica) is not touchy or fretful or resentful; it (Erica) takes no account of the evil done to it (him/her). [It (Erica) pays no attention to a suffered wrong]. It (Erica) does not rejoice at injustice and unrighteousness but rejoices when right and truth prevail. Love (Erica) bears up under anything and everything that comes; love (Erica) is ever ready to believe the best of every person. Its (Erica's) hopes are fadeless under all circumstances, and it (Erica) endures everything [without weakening]. Love (Erica) never fails [never fades out or becomes obsolete or comes to an end].

Lord, I eagerly seek to acquire this love, and I make it my aim and my greatest quest in life. I refuse to harbor malice and resentment in my heart and mind. I resist and cast down all arguments, theories, and reasonings trying to justify wicked thoughts against Your love. Rather, I choose to renew my mind with thoughts about Your love. Thank You that I do not have to dread that someone will do me wrong again, because Your perfect love will rescue me every time. I love everyone, you love everyone, and together, we love everyone.

Lord, Your perfect love working through me casts out fear. Because I know how much You love me and what that love did for me on the cross, I am not afraid. Help me to have a strong understanding of what this means. You said that everyone that loves is born of You, God, and knows You. Help me to truly know You in all my tests, trials, and experiences. When I can act like You when something goes wrong, it shows that I truly know You. Help me to be just like You every day, in Jesus's name. Let my love be without hypocrisy and partiality. Your love inside me does not side with its own little group, but rather it is extravagant and expressive to the whole world. Thank You for giving my heart the capacity and the ability to love the whole world. If I love the least of these, I know that I am really loving You. Thank You for teaching me to love You well.

Help me to see that the love You want me to walk in has been poured into my heart by the Holy Spirit. Lord, because of Your love, I can now be kind and tenderhearted, forgiving everyone just like You forgave us through what Jesus did for us on the cross. I will love others in the same manner with the same measure and the same power that You are, oh Lord.

13

PRAYERS FOR PROTECTION

Exodus 12; Deuteronomy 31:6; Psalm 34:7, 19; 46:1; 57:1; 59:1; 140:4; Psalm 91; Proverbs 2:11; 4:6; Isaiah 41:10; 54:17; Luke 10:19; John 14:6, 27; Romans 8:31, 37–39; Ephesians 6:11–18; Philippians 2:9; 2 Thessalonians 3:3; Hebrews 1:14

My Notes:

God gave us many things to ensure that we are protected from the evil one and his demons. He gave us His precious Holy Spirit; the blood of Jesus; the name of Jesus; power and authority from Jesus; angels of protection; the Word of God; prayer in English and tongues; and praise and worship. Use these tools to fight against the enemy, and you will win every time. For Jesus has the name that is above every name. At Jesus's name, everything on this earth and under the earth has to bow.

Angels are ministering spirits sent to serve and protect us as heirs of God's salvation. Good angels protect us, and bad angels try to steal, kill, and destroy us. The bad angels that have fallen from heaven because of the rebellion of Satan are what we call demons. The Bible is filled with stories and encounters of men with angels. They brought messages of hope, good news, and protection from wars. They were also used to bring judgment. We see the result of the good angels and bad angels in the book of Exodus. Once the children of Israel were finally free of the slavery from Pharaoh, God used angels to protect them in the wilderness.

The children of Israel in Exodus 12 took the blood of a lamb at the command of Moses and put it on a doorpost for protection. The sign that was made with the blood was the Hebrew letter *chet* that represented life.[29] For there is life in the blood. The blood of that lamb was to protect them against the death angel that was coming to kill the firstborn of each family or animal that did not have that symbol. God did not send the death angel, but Satan did. But, God required the shedding of blood from bulls and goats to atone for sins in the Old Testament. However, God put an end to this practice forever when His precious Son Jesus sacrificed His life as the last lamb for all our sins. We can now plead the blood of Jesus or apply His blood symbolically over our lives by words. Jesus's blood not only protects us, but cleanses us from all unrighteousness.

How much more does the blood of Jesus protect us from the evil that is lurking in this world? He is our last and final Passover Lamb. At the name of Jesus, demons must flee. Use His name and the authority we have been given to put Satan and his demons on the run for good. Make sure you symbolically apply the blood of Jesus over all that you possess or reign over through words spoken from your mouth. Plead the blood of Jesus over your family, health, spirit, soul, body, home, cars, jobs, and anything else of importance that you don't want the evil one to attack, harass, or torment. This is how we live protected from all the plots and schemes of our adversary.

---

29   "The Letter Chet," Hebrew for Christians.com, accessed March 4, 2020, https://www.hebrew4christians.com/Grammar/Unit_One/Aleph-Bet/Chet/chet.html.

The Merriam-Webster Dictionary describes the word "adversary" as one that contends with, opposes, or resists: an enemy or opponent. It is one arrayed against you. The devil or Satan is your adversary. He is against us, but the blood of Jesus gives us power or protection against him.[30] The best way to stay prepared, protected, and on guard against our enemy is to stay clothed in the whole armor of God, the whole armor of love. Ephesians 6:11–18 says,

> Put on the whole amour of God, that ye may be able to stand against the wiles of the devil. For we wrestle not against flesh and blood, but against principalities, against powers, against spiritual wickedness in high places. Wherefore take unto you the whole amour of God, that ye may be able to withstand in the evil day, and having done all, to stand. Stand therefore, having your loins girt about with truth, and having on the breastplate of righteousness; And your feet shod with the preparation of the gospel of peace; Above all taking the shield of faith wherewith ye shall be able to quench all the fiery darts of the wicked. And take the helmet of salvation, and the sword of the Spirit, which is the word of God; Praying always with all prayer and supplication in the Spirit, and watching thereunto with all perseverance and supplication for all saints. (KJV)

Note that truth and peace are who Jesus says He is in John 14:6 and verse 27, and righteousness is God's standard of doing and being right that can only be seen in Jesus. The helmet of salvation protects your mind so that it stays focused on God's love and what He did on the cross. Your faith or belief in God without

---

30   *Merriam-Webster*, s.v., "adversary (*n.*)," accessed March 4, 2020, https://www.merriam-webster.com/dictionary/adversary.

seeing Him is a shield that protects from everything in the unseen world. Your sword is the actual Scriptures that you speak. All this is activated and released through prayer. Persevere knowing that Satan and his minions have been disarmed. Let's go to work today defending and protecting ourselves by going on the offense in prayer using the Word of God.

Prayer:

I thank You, almighty God, for protecting me from all hurt, harm, and danger. Let Your angels of protection be encamped about me. I praise You, Lord, that no weapon formed against me shall prosper. Your mighty shield of faith protects me and quenches all the fiery darts of the wicked one. I thank You, Lord, that what the devil meant for evil in my life, You turn around for my good. Bring the devil's plans to kill, steal, and destroy my life to nothing so that they do not work. Nullify all his plans in Jesus's name.

Lord, I truly believe that not one weapon the enemy has shall prosper and that You have given me power and authority on this earth. This power and authority are over all the power the enemy possesses, and *nothing* shall by any means hurt me. For You have made me more than a conqueror. I not only conquer my enemy, but I put all devils and demons on the run. For I rule over them. Your angels, oh Lord, encamp around me as I fear You, and they rescue me every time.

Thank You, Lord, for protecting me with the precious blood of Jesus. Just like the children of Israel put the blood of a lamb on a doorpost to protect them from the death angel, I use the blood of Jesus for protection over all that concerns me and my family. Thank You, Lord, for the ministering spirits (angels) that stand guard over my family. They are battling for my protection, fighting for me, and defending me right now against all of Satan's schemes, devices, attacks, and advances.

Thank You, Lord, for covering me with the whole armor of God. I need the helmet of salvation, the breastplate of righteousness, my loins girded with truth, and my feet shod with the preparation of the gospel of peace. Above all, I take Your shield of faith so that I can quench all the fiery darts of the wicked one. Thank You, Lord, for the sword of the Spirit, which is Your Word that defeats all the lies of the enemy. For Jesus's words are truth and protection against the devil's accusations and lies.

Thank You, Lord, that nothing can ever separate me from Your love. Lord, if You are for me, nothing in this world can be effective against me. Thank You, Lord, no one can be my foe if You are on my side. Lord, I am fully persuaded that in all things, I am more than a conqueror through Jesus who loves me. Your Word says that neither death, nor life, nor angels, nor principalities, nor powers, nor things present, nor things to come, nor height, nor depth, nor any other creature in all creation, shall be able to separate me from the love You have for me in Jesus. This was all found in Christ Jesus's sacrifice on the cross. Jesus, You gave me power and authority over all the power that the enemy thought he had.

Yes, Lord, You are faithful, and You will strengthen and protect me from the evil one. Therefore, I will be strong and courageous and not terrified because You go with me at all times. Your Word says You will never leave or forsake me. Thank You, Lord, for helping me and upholding me by Your right hand.

Father, give me wisdom and knowledge to make the right decisions, for You said discretion will protect me and understanding will guard me. I will not forsake wisdom, for she will watch over me. Lord, I believe that no matter how many troubles I may have, You can and will deliver me out of them all. For I am righteous because of Jesus.

You, oh Lord, are my refuge and strength. You are for me an ever-present help in times of trouble. Thank You, Jesus, for having mercy upon me. I take refuge in You and the shadow of Your wings until all disasters have passed. Keep delivering me from my enemies and keep me safe from the hands of the wicked. Protect me from the violent who devise ways to trip my feet. For You are my fortress against those who are attacking me.

(One of the best prayers for protection is Psalm 91 in the Amplified Bible. Take this passage of Scripture and make it personal by adding your name.)

(Name) who dwells in the secret place of the Most High shall remain stable and fixed under the shadow of the Almighty [Whose power no foe can withstand]. (Name) will say of the Lord, He is my Refuge and my Fortress, my God; on Him, (Name) lean and rely, and in Him, (Name) [confidently] trusts! For [then] He will deliver me from the snare of the fowler and from the deadly pestilence. [Then] He will cover (Name) with His pinions, and under His wings shall I trust and find refuge; His truth and His faithfulness are a shield and a buckler.

(Name) shall not be afraid of the terror of the night, nor of the arrow (evil plots and slanders of the wicked) that flies by day, nor of the pestilence that stalks in darkness, nor of the destruction and sudden death that surprise and lay waste at noonday. A thousand may fall at my side, and ten thousand at my right hand, but it shall not come near (Name). Only a spectator shall (Name) be [myself inaccessible in the secret place of the Most High] as I witness the reward of the wicked. Because (Name) have made the Lord my refuge, and the Most High my dwelling place, there shall no evil befall me, nor any plague or calamity come near my tent.

For He will give His angels [especial] charge over me to accompany and defend and preserve me in all my ways [of obedience and service]. They shall bear (Name) up on their hands, lest (Name) dash [my] foot against a stone. (Name) shall tread upon the lion and adder; the young lion and the serpent shall I trample underfoot. Because (Name) has set his/her love upon me, therefore will I deliver (Name); I will set (Name) on high, because (Name) knows and understands My name [has a personal knowledge of My mercy, love, and kindness—trusts and relies on Me, knowing I will never forsake (Name), no, never]. (Name) shall call upon Me, and I will answer him/her; I will be with him/her in trouble, I will deliver him/her and honor him/her. With long life will I satisfy him/her and show him/her My salvation.

14

PRAYERS FOR LOOSING WHAT IS BOUND

Psalm 146:7; Isaiah 58:6; Jeremiah 40:4; Matthew 7:7 ESV; 16:19; 18:18–20, 27; Luke 13:16; John 14:14; 15:7; Acts 2:24

My Notes:

If things can be bound on earth, then they can be loosed. According to Joe Amaral in *Understanding Jesus Cultural Insights into the Words and Deeds of Christ,* the words "binding" and "loosing" [are] legal terms. They were used to make determinations in laws pertaining to unclear commands in the Torah. To 'bind' something meant to forbid it, and to 'loose' something meant to permit it."[31] The teachers of Jesus's day would hear arguments and make determinations about what they would allow or forbid concerning interpretations of Jewish laws. Therefore, the term "loose" meant that they were allowing an activity to be done. However, the Amplified Bible Classic Edition says "loose" means to let things go free or to declare them to be lawful because they are lawful in heaven.[32] Jesus taught in Matthew 18:18, "Truly I tell you, whatever you forbid and declare to be improper and unlawful on earth must be what is already forbidden in heaven,

---

31   Amaral, *Understanding.*

32   *Merriam-Webster,* s.v., "loose (*v.*)," accessed March 4, 2020, https://www. merriam-webster.com/dictionary/loose.

and whatever you permit and declare proper and lawful on earth must be what is already permitted in heaven" (AMPC). It is our job to loose the things of God in our lives every day. We can loose our power, joy, peace, love, health, the favor of God, strength, prosperity, and more to work every day.

Jesus told people to loose Lazarus from his grave clothes when He raised him from the dead in John 11. He told them to loose him and let him go. Jesus wants us loosed from death, hell, and the grave every day. Jesus always wants us to be loosed or freed from *all* the fiery darts of the wicked one.

You can't just ask for whatever you want in prayer. You must ask for what conforms to God's will and purpose. He will not give you another woman's husband or another man's wife, even if you believe. That is absolutely against God's will as stated in His Word.

Prayer:

Father, I loose your glory to fall and be at work in my life. I loose Jesus's power, peace, prosperity, healing, and joy to work in me daily. Thank You, Lord, for helping me to fast and break the rule and control of the flesh. The fast that You have chosen helps us to loose the bands of wickedness, undo heavy burdens, to let the oppressed go free, and to break every yoke. I am grateful You are loosing me this day from every chain and yoke of bondage in my life. For You are the God who executes judgment for the oppressed and gives food to the hungry. You loose every prisoner locked up in death.

Thank You, Lord, for loosing us and forgiving us from every debt and every infirmity. Thank You, Lord, for loosing me from every area where Satan has tried to bind me.

Thank You for loosing and releasing the glory of God! Your manifested presence is showing up so that we see your power loose us from the works of Satan in our everyday lives. I loose Jesus's peace, joy, strength, power, victory, and success in Jesus's name. I loose the angels of God to go to work on my behalf. Glory to You, oh Lord, for raising me up and loosing the pains of death and destruction.

Jesus, You said in John 14:14, that whatever I ask in Your name, You will do it.

(Remember that Jesus's name is not just His name. His name is what He says and does. This is how you know people on earth. Just because you know a person's name does not mean that you know them. You find out about them when you spend time with them, getting to know them. Therefore, Jesus said whatever we ask in His name, He will do it. We see that His name is His love, power, character, and authority. Whatever you ask in His name, He said He *will* do it, not *maybe* He will. My pastor Robert Scales taught me this. This teaching changed my life.)

John 15:7 says if I abide in Jesus and His words abide in me, then I could ask what I will, and it would be done for me. Lord, I abide in You, and Your words abide in me. Therefore, I ask for _____ (fill in the blank), and I thank You, Lord, that it shall be done unto me.

Lord, Your Word says to ask, and it will be given to me; seek, and I will find; knock, and it will be opened to me. Lord, I am asking for _____ (fill in the blank). I am seeking You about _____ (fill in the blank). Thank You, Lord, _____ (fill in the blank) will be opened unto me in Jesus's name.

Thank You, Lord, for loosing me from all of Satan's works. I am no longer in bondage and locked up in death. I have been redeemed or loosed from curses. I loose the blessing of Abraham to be at work in my life every day. My mind is loosed from the control of evil spirits. I have the mind of Christ, and I am sober and calm in my thinking because You love me.

15

PRAYERS FOR PROSPERITY AND FINANCES

Genesis 22:18; Joshua 1:8; Psalm 23:1; 37:25; 112:2–3; Proverbs 10:4; 11:25; 13:4, 22; 21:5; 22:29; Isaiah 1:19; 48:17; Matthew 6:10; Luke 4:18; John 14:14; 15:7; Acts 20:35; 2 Corinthians 8:9,14; 9:6–11; Galatians 3:13, 14–29; Philippians 4:19; 2 Peter 1:3; 3 John 1:2

My Notes:

Understanding prosperity means understanding Psalms 23. The Lord is our Shepherd and we shall not want. A shepherd takes full care of the sheep. Sheep won't even go for water unless the shepherd leads them to still waters.

We have already discussed Galatians 3:13 in another section. But what is worth emphasizing is the fact that Jesus redeemed us or purchased our freedom from the curse of poverty. Poverty was and will always be a curse because it does not represent who God is. One of the names for God is El Shaddai. This means He is the God of more than enough. Just being enough would be great, but He is *more* than enough. God is the all sufficient one. King David had this revelation when he stated, "I have been young, and now am old; yet have I not seen the righteous forsaken, nor his seed begging bread" (KJV). Abraham also had this knowledge about God.

In Genesis 22:18, God told Abraham that through his offspring, all nations in the earth would be blessed, because he had obeyed God. Thank you, Abraham, for your obedience. Abraham and his nephew Lot became so wealthy and blessed that they had to split up and go separate ways because their cattle were too great. Leroy Thompson once taught a sermon about prosperity. He mentioned that the word "blessed" means to be empowered to prosper. God empowers us to prosper in many ways, such as starting a business, giving dreams, revelations, inspiration, ideas, opportunities, jobs, other people, and more. God also wants us to prosper in more areas than in just our finances. God told His beloved in 3 John 1:2 that "I wish above all things that thou mayest prosper and be in health, even as thy soul prospereth" (KJV). When we accept Jesus in our hearts, we receive the Holy Spirit as our Helper, and then He leads and guides us into our wealthy place.

The Bible says that we are joint heirs with Christ once we receive Him into our hearts as Lord and Savior. This means that you have equal access—the same as Jesus—to all that heaven provides. No one in heaven is suffering or struggling to survive. God is prosperity, not lack or shortage. In fact, God will always be too much and more than enough. Jesus taught the disciples that they could pray for things on earth to be as they are in heaven in Matthew 6:10. No one is broke or struggling to make it in heaven, and neither should I.

Prayer:

Thank You, Lord, that Christ became poor so that we, through His poverty, might be rich. I thank You, Lord, that I am abundantly supplied. Lord, I thank You that You provide seed to the sower and You multiply our seed sown.

For You, oh Lord, are my shepherd, and I shall not want. Thank You, Lord, for supplying all my needs, according to your riches in glory by Christ Jesus. According to this, Father, I only have one need, and that is Christ. Lord Jesus, if I have You, I have everything I need. Lord, You promised that Your divine power has given me everything that pertains to life and godliness when I received Jesus as my Lord. Therefore, I declare that *all* my needs are met in Jesus's name.

Thank You, Lord, for too much, overflow, abundance, affluence, influence, and wealth. Because of You, I have an abundant flow or supply. Thank You, Lord, for showing and teaching me how to have an influx of income coming from multiple streams. Therefore, I bind the spirit of lack and insufficiency in Jesus's name. The spirit of poverty will not steal and rob me of what is rightfully mine as a child of God. Thank You, ministering spirits, for going to get my money from the north, south, east, and west in Jesus's name.

Thank You, Lord, for the privilege of prayer. You said if I abide in You and Your words abide in me, then I can ask what I will, and it shall be done for me. Lord, I abide in You because Jesus's words are living in my heart. Therefore, I am asking You to prosper me in every way, and You promised that it will be done for me. You said whatever I ask in Your name, Jesus, You would do it. I know Your name is your love, power, character, and authority. So in the authority of Christ, I command the money to come to me now in Jesus's name.

Lord, You promised that if I meditate on Your Word day and night and observe to do it, then I will make my way prosperous, and then I will have good success. I am meditating on Your promises right now. Thank You, Lord, for teaching me to deal wisely with my finances and the affairs of life. Train me in business so that I may have good success in all that I do.

Thank You, Lord, for teaching me to be a good steward of all You have given me. Help me not to be lazy or procrastinate, but rather let me be diligent in all things. For You said, "He who deals with a slack hand becomes poor, but the hand of the diligent makes themselves rich." Lord, don't let my mind be like a sluggard who desires things and has nothing. But rather let my mind be diligent so that it can be made fat. For the thoughts of the diligent tend only to plenteousness. Help me to be diligent and keep my mind on what You have told me to do that brings plenteousness and security. I need You to make me diligent in business so that I can stand before kings.

Thank You, Lord, for an excellent spirit. Lord, I will not con, cheat, steal, or manipulate to get what I want in life. Instead, I will praise my miracle-working God for performing miracles on my behalf. I expect that something good is going to happen to me today. I am expecting a miracle today. Thank You, Lord, for divine connections.

Thank You, Jesus, that You are my Redeemer. You purchased my freedom from poverty, debt, and lack. You, oh Lord, teach me to profit, and You lead me in the way I should go.

Thank You, Lord, that the wealth of the wicked is finding its way into my hands today. You said it was laid up for the righteous. I am grateful that it is no longer laid up but coming to me now quickly and speedily. Money, move *now* in my direction in Jesus's name.

Thank You that I get to leave an inheritance of moral stability and wealth to my children. Thank You, Lord, that I am the generation of the upright and I am blessed. I declare that wealth and riches are in my house in Jesus's name. I thank You, Lord, that the blessing of Abraham is upon me and my family in Jesus's name.

Poverty is a satanic anointing that I will not accept. I thank You, Lord, for the anointing to prosper and be blessed. Your anointing breaks yokes and removes burdens. Your anointing has broken the yoke of poverty, debt, and lack off my life forever.

Thank You, Jesus, that my surplus will meet another's needs and wants, and someone else's surplus can help meet my needs and the needs of others. You bring equality for us all. I am grateful for too much and overflow so that I may help send the gospel all over the world. For this is the true purpose of having wealth.

Help me, Lord, not to be stingy. Your Word says, "He that sows sparingly will reap sparingly, but if I give bountifully, I will reap bountifully so that blessings may come to others." Thank You, Lord, for making all grace abound toward me as I sow and give to others. Thank You, Lord, for multiplying my seed sown back to me one-hundred-fold.

Thank You, Lord, that as I am willing and obedient to do what You say in every area, I now get to eat the good of the land every day.

Thank You, Lord, that those who bless others are abundantly blessed and those who help others are helped. I choose to bless and give so that I can be abundantly blessed. Lord, Your Word says, "I am *more* blessed to give than to receive." Lord, I will give from my heart with an abundance of joy and make You happy. I do not give out of compulsion but from a place of gratefulness for all you have done for and given to me.

16

PRAYERS FOR GETTING RID OF FEAR

Psalm 23:4; 34:4; 112:7–8; Proverbs 1:33; Isaiah 41:10; 43:1; Luke 1:74–75; 10:19; John 14:6, 27; 16:33; Philippians 2:5–8; 2 Timothy 1:7; 1 John 4:18

My Notes:

I read an article on fear that said, "God actually commands us not to fear, or worry. The phrase "fear not" is used at least 80 times in the Bible, most likely because He knows the enemy uses fear to decrease our hope and limit our victories."[33] Specifically, God said in Isaiah 43:1, "Don't fear, for I have redeemed you; I have called you by name; you are Mine." When you belong to God, you do not need to fear because He will take care of you and protect you from all hurt, harm, and danger.

This is why the acronym for fear is False Evidence Appearing Real.[34] Satan and his demons often use lies to scare you, but they are never the truth that is in Christ Jesus. Jesus said that His words are truth. He is *the* way, *the* truth, and *the* life. He is not

---

33   Jessica Kastner, "Top 4 Biblical Promises that Banish Fear," *The Christian Broadcasting Network*, accessed July 31, 2020, https://www1.cbn.com/top-4-biblical-promises-banish-fear.

34   The acronym has been around for years and is commonly used. As such, a specific attribution could not be located.

a way to get to God; He is the *only* way to get to God and know Him accurately. Fear will do its best to come against you and make you doubt, question, waver, or be afraid of God not being there or coming through for you. Fear will try to paralyze you so that you cannot function or move with confidence in what Jesus taught, said, and did.

Also, we previously discussed that fear is a form of faith but faith in the wrong thing. You must place your trust and confidence in the promises of the Word of God and not in the circumstances of life. In addition, God did not give a spirit of fear. He only gives love, power, and a sound mind. A person who has a sound of mind does not give way to anxiety, upsetting situations, or hysterical thoughts but rather controls their mind and keeps these thoughts in check. This person knows how to discipline themselves to think about Jesus and have the mind of Christ and not the world.

When we live free from fear, we are rooted and grounded in love. First John 4:18 shows us that perfect love casts out fear because fear has torment. The Amplified Bible says, "There is no fear in love [dread does not exist], but full-grown (complete, perfect) love turns fear out of doors and expels every trace of terror! For fear brings with it the thought of punishment, and [so] he who is afraid has not reached the full maturity of love [is not yet grown into love's complete perfection]."

Prayer:

Help us, Lord, to distinguish between the devil's accusations, facts, and lies and Jesus's truth and reality. Thank You, Lord, that You have not given me a spirit of fear, but of love, power, and a sound mind. I know that a sound mind means a mind of discipline and self-control. Help me, Father, to have discipline in my thinking.

I refuse to allow fear to paralyze me so that I cannot function and move. I thank You, Lord, that Your perfect love casts fear out of my life and expels every trace of terror. I am not afraid, Lord, that You don't love me and won't come through for me. I am not afraid. I thank You, Lord, for setting me free from evil forebodings or expectations of danger. I believe instead that something good is going to happen to me today. I am expecting a miracle today. I will not be afraid of evil tidings because my heart is fixed, trusting in You, oh Lord.

Lord, even if I walk through a valley where there is a shadow of death, I will fear no evil against me. For You are with me, and Your rod and Your staff comfort me. Thank You for not leaving me alone. Lord, Your Word says that, if I listen to You, I will dwell safely, be secure, and have no fear of evil. I choose to listen to You today.

I am full of love and not afraid.

I am full of courage and not a coward.

I am bold as a lion and not shy.

I am full of self-confidence and not timid.

I am full of favor with God and man and not fawning (trying to gain favor by acting humble).

I am facing problems head on with the power of the Holy Spirit and not craven (yielding or giving up).

I am walking in power and authority over all the power that the enemy possesses, and nothing shall by any means hurt me in this life. I am not cringing or in fear of being hurt.

Thank You, Lord, for my calm and well-balanced mind. I refuse to be of two minds, wavering back and forth. I settle the issue today that You are in love with me and Your love comes to do something about what I am going through in life.

Thank You, Lord, for loving me and satisfying me with Your love. I see You, Lord, as bigger than anything that I will ever face in this life. You are my miracle-working God.

Thank You, Lord, that I do not fear in life because You are with me. I am never alone. I refuse to be dismayed, for You are my God and will strengthen me in all things. I sought You, Lord, and You heard me and delivered me from all my fears. Lord, You grant unto me to be delivered from the hand of my enemies so that I can serve You without fear. Also, because my heart is established, I will not be afraid until I see my desire upon my enemies. Instead, I will live in holiness and righteousness before You all the days of my life. Glory to God, I am free from all *fear*!

17

PRAYERS FOR PEACE AND THE REMOVAL OF STRESS, WORRY, OR DEPRESSION

Psalm 119:165; Isaiah 9:6; 26:3; 35:10; 61:3; Matthew 11:28–30; John 14:27; 16:33; Romans 14:17; 15:13; 2 Corinthians 5:7; Philippians 4:6–8; 10:3–5; James 1:2–3; 1 Peter 5:7

My Notes:

Peace or *shalom* means to be whole or complete. It means to be entire, wanting nothing. If you have perfect peace, there is nothing broken or missing in your life. You will experience wholeness in every area. The encyclopedia describes peace as success, fulfillment, wholeness, harmony, security, and well-being.[35] However, Bible Study Tools describes peace as a personality free from internal and external strife.[36] It means to live well. Bible Study Tools says that shalom addresses four areas:

1. Wholeness of life or body (health)

2. Right relationships or harmony between parties or people. This often comes through a covenant of peace.

---

35   *Strong's Concordance*, Bible hub.com, "7965. Shalom," accessed March 4, 2020, https://biblehub.com/hebrew/7965.htm.

36   *Baker's Evangelical Dictionary of Bible Theology,* Bible Study Tools.com, "peace," accessed March 4, 2020, https://www.biblestudytools.com/dictionary/peace/.

3. Prosperity, success, or fulfillment

4. Victory over one's enemies or the absence of war[37]

As I previously stated, the Hebrew word for peace is *shalom*. The encyclopedia describes shalom as the "realm where chaos is not allowed to enter."[38] Chaos is understood as sickness, war, social strife, or the violation of a covenant. The Jews use the word *shalom* to greet each other and when they are saying goodbye. It is a blessing on the one to whom it was spoken. They say, "May your life be filled with health, prosperity, and victory."[39] Shalom also expresses the meaning of completeness and safety. Shalom can also be a question. It means, "Is everything okay or well with you in every area of your life?"

One method for obtaining shalom is coming unto Jesus. He taught in Matthew 11:28-30 to, "Come unto me, all ye that labour and are heavy laden, and I will give you rest. Take my yoke upon you, and learn of me; for I am meek and lowly in heart: and ye shall find rest unto your souls. For my yoke is easy, and my burden is light (KJV)." Therefore, if you want to have total peace and be free from stress and worry, you must come to Jesus and learn from Him.

The Merriam-Webster Dictionary describes a yoke as a bar or frame that is attached to the heads or necks of two work animals, like oxen, so that they can pull a heavy load together.[40] It can also

---

37   Ibid.

38   Encyclopedia.com, "Peace," accessed March 4, 2020, https://www.encyclopedia.com/religion/encyclopedias-almanacs-transcripts-and-maps/peace-bible.

39   *Baker's*, "peace," https://www.biblestudytools.com/dictionary/peace/.

40   *Merriam-Webster*, s.v., "yoke (*n.*)," accessed March 4, 2020, https://www.merriam-webster.com/dictionary/yoke.

be an arched device laid on the neck of a defeated person. In Jesus, we are never defeated, and He helps us through every problem with power and victory. However, Jesus still has a yoke. But, the yoke of Jesus is not one of oppression, depression, worry, or stress. His yoke is wholesome, useful, and good, and not harsh, hard, sharp, or pressing.

Further, Jesus's yoke is comfortable, gracious, and pleasant, and His burden is light and easy to carry. Jesus wants to help us carry our heavy loads in life. He does not add to the difficulties life can bring, but He destroys the harsh, cruel yoke of the devil off us. Jesus said He had a light burden. A minor burden for a Christian might be believing by faith when you cannot see the end result. Sometimes, people struggle with believing by faith. For we walk by faith and not by sight. If we pay attention to our physical senses, we will not be in faith. Faith never considers how a situation looks or feels. Faith only considers what Jesus had to say about the subject. For faith is Jesus's words in action. All of us can carry a light burden of believing in the midst of what looks impossible when Jesus helps us along the way.

Great news: Jesus is the Prince of Peace! He gives us freedom from disquieting or oppressive thoughts and crazy emotions.

Prayer:

Thank You, Jesus, that You are my peace. You told me in John 14:27 that You left me Your peace (AMP). You told me not to allow myself to be agitated, frustrated, or disturbed. I thank You, Jesus, that I have the mind of Christ. I cast down every thought of inadequacy, stress, worry, oppression, and depression. I refuse to think about what brings negativity, doubt, or unbelief. But rather I choose to think about what is lovely, pure, just, honest, and of a good report. I bring every thought captive into the obedience of Christ. I cast down every high thing that exalts itself against the knowledge of God's love for me and others. I refuse to fret or be anxious about the things of this world, especially what I cannot fix or change. Instead, I pray about everything and remember to stay thankful in every circumstance. Lord, I believe that You have given me power and authority in every battle I face. This power helps me to overcome every situation, circumstance, distress, or pressure sent by Satan.

Lord, I know that You told me that in this world, there would be tests, trials, tribulations, and distresses. But You told me to be of good cheer because You have overcome the world and deprived it of power to harm me. You have conquered everything I'm facing on the cross. I believe Your love will never fail me, fade away, or come to an end.

Father, Jesus taught us to come to Him when we were overburdened and heavy laden. He promised to give us rest. I thank You, Jesus, that I am coming to You today to partake of Your rest and to learn of You. The more I learn of You, the more I walk in victory because You never fail. Thank You, Jesus, for relieving, easing, and refreshing my mind from the cares of this world.

Jesus, You promised that if I truly learned of You, I could take Your yoke in life. Your yoke is easy, and Your burdens are light. I take Your yoke and allow You to carry my load today. I refuse to try and handle things in my own strength ever again. You said the Father entrusted You with *all* things and You want to show them to me. I will allow You to do Your job today. Show me how to release all my cares and concerns now.

Lord, I cast *all* my cares on You, for You care for me. I give You all my anxieties, mistakes, problems, worries, concerns, fears, failures, and setbacks once and for all. I will not take them back. Thank You for caring for me affectionately and watchfully. I refuse to keep any cares or negative emotions. Thank You, Lord, for keeping me in perfect peace as I keep my mind stayed on You.

I thank You, Lord, that I keep Your law of love in John 13:34. Therefore, I have great peace because I live in nothing being wrong with myself or others. Lord, I give You praise that You are removing all chaos from my life in Jesus's name. I am complete in You. I am whole and entire, wanting nothing.

Thank You, Lord, for giving me the oil of joy for mourning and the garment of praise for the spirit of heaviness. Lord, help me to consider it pure joy when I face many kinds of trials. I know that the testing of my faith produces perseverance. I am grateful that You are the God of hope and You fill me with joy and peace in believing as I trust in You. I overflow with hope by the power of the Holy Spirit.

Lord, because You have rescued me from depression, worry, and fear, I now sing with the everlasting joy that crowns my head. Gladness and joy overtake me now in the name of Jesus. I command sorrow and sighing to flee away in Jesus's name. I am thankful that I am in Your kingdom of righteousness, peace, and joy in the Holy Spirit.

18

PRAYERS FOR REMOVING PRIDE

Proverbs 3:6; 11:2; 12:15; 13:10; 16:5,18; 18:12; 27:2; 29:23; Isaiah 5:15; Matthew 23:11–12; Mark 10:43–45; John 15:5; Romans 12:3; Galatians 3:9–11 (MSG), 13; Philippians 2:3, 8; 4:13; James 4:6–7; 1 Peter 5:6–7; 2 Peter 1:3; 1 John 2:15–16

My Notes:

Living in pride is not just about looking down on others. Pride at its core is when we have a really high estimation of our own self-importance without Jesus as the source of the elevation. Because of our own self-importance, we begin to see others as less important and therefore irrelevant. For example, I once heard Keith Moore preach in a sermon that even cutting a person off while they are speaking is a form of pride. We sometimes think that what we have to say is so vital that others should just shut up and listen. However, we want to imitate and emulate Jesus, who humbled Himself as a servant. He taught in Matthew 23:11–12 that "he that is greatest among you shall be your servant, and whosoever shall exalt himself shall be abased; and he that shall humble himself shall be exalted" (KJV). Living this verse requires us to pretend that we are a waiter in a restaurant. My pastor Robert Scales taught our congregation to take our orders from Jesus and

His teachings. We are to see what Jesus wants us to do in life and then bring only that back to Him with joy and without attitudes.

One of the greatest areas of pride is when we do not bow our knees to Jesus's lordship. This means that we do not willingly give Him permission to rule and dominate our wills, which makes us exalt ourselves or our own ability. When people start to exalt themselves, they begin to live in their own strength, independent of God's help. Galatians 3:9–11 puts it this way.

> So those who live by faith are blessed along with Abraham, who lived by faith-this is no new doctrine! And that means that anyone who tries to live by his own effort, independent of God, is doomed to failure. Scripture backs this up: "Utterly cursed is every person who fails to carry out every detail written in the Book of the law." The obvious impossibility of carrying out such a moral program should make it plain that no one can sustain a relationship with God that way. The person who lives in right relationship with God does it by embracing what God arranges for him. Doing things for God is the opposite of entering into what God does for you. (MSG)

This is why Jesus redeemed us or purchased our freedom from the curse of the law or doing things in our own strength without Him.

Further, the Scriptures say that we "can do all things through Christ who strengthens us" (Philippians 4:13 KJV). We must not live in spiritual arrogance but realize just how much we need Jesus and the Holy Spirit to speak and tell us what to do in every situation. If we are acknowledging the Lord in all of our ways, then we are submitted and trusting God to lead and guide us and not ourselves. If we are guiding ourselves, we are in pride. Therefore, we can either humble ourselves and admit our dependence on God to make it, or we will watch the test and trials of life bring us low. Isaiah 5:15 says, "The mean man shall be brought down, and the mighty man shall be humbled, and the eyes of the lofty shall be humbled" (KJV).

Even Jesus, who was found in fashion as a man, humbled Himself and became obedient unto the death of the cross. Jesus was submitted and dependent upon the Father to tell Him where to go, what to say, and what to do while on the earth. A key here is submitting and coming under Jesus's authority, which helps us to resist the devil and then he has to flee. You can find proof of that in James 4:7. With this understanding, we can easily see that the measure to which I yield to Jesus and the Holy Spirit's leadership, lordship, and guidance, will be the degree or level of victory that I walk in daily.

Prayer:

Father, I know that without You, I can do nothing. Holy Spirit, I need You to lead and guide me through this day. Don't let me make any decisions independent of Your help. I give You permission to rule and dominate my spirit, soul, and body. Don't let pride have its way in me today.

Father, Your Word says to let another man praise me and not my own mouth because my pride can bring me low. When pride comes, it will bring with it shame and strife. Instead of these working in my life, help me to be lowly and humble so that I can have wisdom. For when Your wisdom works in us, we know that we are truly well-advised. Lord, help me not to think of myself more highly than I ought to think, but rather soberly as You have given me a measure of faith.

I refuse to try and be great. I am believing in who You have made me. Your Word says that if I desire to be great, then I should be a minister and servant of all. Lord, show me today who I can serve so that You may be glorified and exalted and not me. Jesus, You are my example. You did not come to be served but to serve and give your life as a ransom for many. Therefore, I take on the attitude of a servant. Father, just like a waiter, it is my honor to hear what orders You want to give me today. I will hear and bring them back to You with joy.

I renounce the spirit of pride and self-righteousness from working in my life in Jesus's name. Father, I know that pride comes before destruction and a haughty spirit before a fall. Your Word also says that pride is an abomination or one of the things that you truly hate. So I am asking You to change me and help me to never walk in pride. I thank You, Jesus, for setting me free from the lust of the flesh, the lust of the eyes, and the pride of life. I will not boast of my own possessions. For I know that Your divine power has blessed me with all things that pertain to life and godliness. Jesus, I am 100 percent dependent upon You for all things.

Don't let me boast of myself but rather of Your goodness and mercy. May You, oh Lord, receive all the praise, honor, and glory for anything good that comes as a result of Your wisdom, power, and goodness working in my life. I live for Your glory and to bring You praise and honor every day.

I bow my knees to Your lordship and admit my dependency on You, Jesus, to make it through this day. Not my will, but Your will be done through me. I humble myself in my own eyes. I demote and lower myself under Your mighty hand, Lord God, so that You may exalt me in due time. I thank You, Lord, for helping me to keep the proper estimation of myself in line with Christ's ability operating through me. Pride goes before destruction and a haughty spirit before a fall. Help me, Holy Spirit, not to fall today.

Thank You, Lord, that You give more grace through the power of the Holy Spirit to those who do not walk in pride but remain humble. You resist the proud, and I do not want to be resisted in life. Do not let me be reduced to my own human ability. Let me receive more and more grace or power of the Holy Spirit to help me in my times of need. I see that as I submit and bow my knees to Your lordship, I can resist the devil and watch him flee.

Oh, what joy it is to know that Satan is running from me in terror when I constantly do what You say, Jesus, and stay out of pride. For this, Lord Jesus, I give You praise. I cannot do these things in my own strength. Therefore, I am expecting the Holy Spirit to bring me more and more of God's ability to do for me and in me what I cannot do for myself. I humble myself by casting all my cares on You. Help me to not be a fool by thinking I'm right in my own eyes. Instead, I choose to listen to wise counsel and become wise.

Holy Spirit, help me not to do anything out of selfish ambition or vain conceit. Rather in humility, let me value others above myself. Lord, where there is strife, there is pride, but Your wisdom is found in those who take advice. I choose to take godly counsel on this day. I will not be a fool and establish my own way. Amen.

19

PRAYERS FOR NIGHTTIME

Job 33:15; Psalm 16:7; 17:3; 121:4; Proverbs 3:24, 26; Isaiah 1:18; Jeremiah 1:12; Matthew 11:28; Ephesians 4:26; 6:10; 1 Peter 2:24; 1 John 1:7; 3:5, 8; 5:21

My Notes:

Psalm 121:4 says, "Indeed, he who watches over Israel never slumbers or sleeps" (KJV). Knowing that God watches over us night and day is very comforting. He cares about us even when we are sleeping. This is why we should never forget to pray over ourselves before going to bed. Job showed us in the Word of God that "He [God] speaks in dreams, visions of the night, when deep sleep falls on people as they lie in their beds" (Job 33:15 KJV). Because the busyness of life calms down at night, God has the opportunity to speak to His creation in a still, small voice. He will give you a dream or talk right to your spirit man. This is why "You can go to bed without fear, you can lie down and sleep soundly , , , , for the Lord is your security" (Proverbs 3:24, 26 KJV).

We should "bless the Lord who guides [us]; even at night [our] heart instructs [us]" (Psalm 16:7). Therefore, I can boldly say, "You have tested my thoughts and examined my heart in the night . . . I am determined not to sin in what I say" (Psalm 17:3). We can see an opportunity at night in these verses to clear our minds from any and all sin and negativity that occurred during that day. We then do a purge of these things by asking for forgiveness and asking the Holy Spirit how to not stumble or fall for the next day. Then plead the blood of Jesus over your mind and family and ask God to send angels of protection to watch over you while you sleep. We plead the blood of Jesus over ourselves and all our possessions. This will help to protect your home from invaders and your mind from evil spirits who want to bring bad dreams and disrupt your sleep.

Also remember to forgive everyone before the day ends. We should never go to bed angry. A favorite verse of Scripture that people often quote is Ephesians 4:26. "Be ye angry, and sin not: let not the sun go down upon your wrath" (KJV). When there is nothing wrong, there will be peace. There is nothing like going to bed in perfect peace. When people go to bed angry, they toss and turn all night.

We should never just rush off to sleep without prayer. Take the time to reflect on what was good and bad throughout the day and then focus your attention on that in prayer. If you had failure, great tests, trials, or troubles with people, then ask the Holy Spirit for help in these areas. Then, you will see yourself improving day by day by becoming more like Christ. He helps us become more than a conqueror as well as an overcomer as He gives you wisdom and knowledge to make the right decisions on a daily basis.

Prayer:

Thank You, Lord, that You are the God who never sleeps or slumbers. Therefore, You are constantly watching over me and protecting me from all hurt, harm, and danger. Forgive us of our sins and wash us in Your blood from what was not pleasing to you on this day. We are so thankful Lord, that You have protected us today. Thank You for Jesus, who was sent to loose, dissolve, and destroy the works the devil has done. I am thankful that Jesus was manifested to take away our sins. Keep changing us into Your very own image that we may inwardly share Your likeness. Help us to keep walking in the light as You are in the light, Jesus, so that we can fellowship one with another. Then Your blood will keep us cleansed from all unrighteousness.

Thank You, Lord, for blessing our sleep. Send Your angels to watch over us as we sleep. May we wake up revived, refreshed, and ready to worship You another day. May we be renewed, quickened, and recharged from the strenuous activities of this day. May Your angels quicken and make alive every joint, cell, organ, and tissue. Strengthen our bodies, bones, and immune systems while we sleep. I bind every spirit of sickness, disease, and infirmity in Jesus's name. With the stripes that wounded Jesus, we are healed and made whole in our bodies.

I thank You, Lord, for more of Your grace to resist evil tendencies. Set us free from idols and anything else that wants to take first place in our hearts that is due to You. If we have committed any sins today, cleanse us from all unrighteousness. Father, we ask You to speak to us concerning our lives while we sleep. Show us your plans, purposes, and pursuits. Whether it is a dream or a vision, show us the next steps to take for Your glory. You are magnificent and amazing.

Jesus, thank You for watching over Your Word to perform it in my life. The entrance of Your word into the dark places of my heart gives me light and hope to keep going another day. I choose to give Your Word first place in my life and not my selfish desires.

Because of Your love, Lord, I do not let the sun go down upon my wrath. I loose everybody and myself from everything that has happened on this day. I choose to release everything to You. Holy Spirit, help me to cast all my cares upon You, for You care for me affectionately and watchfully.

Thank You, Lord, for sweet, peaceful, and restful sleep. May Your angels watch over our hearts and minds as we sleep. Thank You for sweet dreams. I bind all night terrors in Jesus's name. Cover us with the whole armor of God and the precious blood of Jesus. No weapon formed against us as we sleep shall prosper. Amen.

20

PRAYERS FOR BINDING EVIL SPIRITS

Isaiah 57:14; Matthew 18:18; Luke 10:19; 2 Corinthians 10:5; Ephesians 1:19–22; 3:19; 6:12; Colossians 2:15; 1 Thessalonians 5:23; Hebrews 4:12; 1 John 4:3; Revelation 12:11

My Notes:

As I previously mentioned, you are spirit, soul, and body. You are a speaking spirit being, with a soul (which is your mind, will, and emotions), and we live in a body. The real you is the spirit inside your body. Your body or flesh is just your house, not the real you. We need to take a look at how evil spirits work or operate through these three components of man. They will try to harass, possess, oppress, or depress a person's human spirit, soul (mind), or body. A person can also obsess in his or her thoughts because of demonic influences.

Evil spirits cannot possess the spirit of a born-again child of God. When a person invites Jesus to live in their heart, their spirit man becomes sealed until the day of Christ. Evil spirits can harass Christians by oppressing their minds or bodies. They do this by weighing you down with cares, unforgiveness, sicknesses, harassing thoughts, or mind games. Devils and demons will also try and cause you to obsess in your thinking or soul while oppressing you in your body or flesh. One of their strongest tactics is to continually bombard a mind with a destructive thought pattern.

These destructive thought patterns can play in your mind like a broken record on a continual loop. They will do this until the child of God begins to resist the thoughts and cast them down in Jesus's name, or by praising and worshipping God which lifts any spirit of heaviness. Second Corinthians 10:4–5 gives us the proper method for tackling harassing thoughts, depression, strongholds, and bad mindsets. We call these a diseased soul because the mind is truly sick. However, 2 Corinthians instructs us first that "the weapons of our warfare are not physical [weapons of flesh and blood], but they are mighty before God for the overthrow and destruction of strongholds, [Inasmuch as we] refute arguments and theories and reasonings and every proud and lofty thing that sets itself up against the [true] knowledge of God; and we lead every thought and purpose away captive into the obedience of Christ (the Messiah, the Anointed One)" (AMPC).

To do this, we must first learn to judge our thoughts to see whether they are in line with what Jesus taught, said, and did for us on the cross. If they are not, then begin to renounce the bad thoughts and tell them to get out of your mind in Jesus's name. Oftentimes, our thoughts are influenced by evil spirits that want to control us by taking over our mind. Reading and quoting the Word of God helps us to distinguish between the voices influencing our thoughts. We can line up our thoughts with Scripture to see who is talking to us: Jesus and the Holy Spirit or an evil spirit. Who is talking to you today? If it is an evil spirit and not the voice of the Good Shepherd, bind it in Jesus's name and tell it to get out of your mind and body.

Keep in mind that reading the Word of God replaces the destructive thoughts trying to lock you up in death in your thinking. This is the only thing that can make negative thoughts leave besides worship. Our job is to daily bind every evil spirit and their operation from working in us in Jesus's name. Remember that to bind means to lock up things or to declare them to be unlawful on earth because they are unlawful in heaven.

Prayer:

Father, Your Word says, that "whatsoever I bind (declare to be improper and unlawful) on earth, shall be bound (already forbidden) in heaven."

Therefore, I renounce and bind the spirit of pride and self-righteousness from working in my life. I bind the spirit of lust, lies, manipulation, poverty, and lack. I thank You, Lord, that I have more than enough. I bind the spirit of insufficiency and not enough. I have too much. I bind the spirit of unforgiveness and strife from working in my life. I refuse to be mad and angry at people or myself.

I bind the spirit of witchcraft and rebellion from working in my life. I bind the spirit of homosexuality. I will not listen to the lies that these voices have told me. I refuse to obey their suggestions or promptings in Jesus's name. Lord, through Your power, I will cast down every wrong thought, feeling, and emotion that is inconsistent with the words that came from Jesus's lips. Your Word tells me to bring every thought captive into the obedience of Christ. If Jesus did not teach it, I will not accept it. I refuse to have arguments, theories, and reasonings concerning the Word of God. I will submit to the Holy Spirit's leadership and guidance in every challenge or decision that I face.

Father, I refuse to be right, but I allow Jesus's words about life to make me right. Jesus's words tell me who You made me to be in Christ. The world will not define who I am because I am a new creature in Christ Jesus. The old parts of me have passed away, and I have become new. I am new in my words and deeds.

Lord, don't let evil spirits teach me. I bind every seducing spirit and the doctrines that demons teach in Jesus's name. I bind the spirit deception, manipulation, corruption, hatred, and strife that tries to rule down through our leaders. I bind the antichrist spirit and command you to loose my money in Jesus's name. I bind every antichrist spirit and anything against Jesus that does not confess that Jesus came in the flesh.

I bind every hindering spirit that is trying to slow down or stop the progress of what God wants done in the earth. Satan will not hinder, delay, sabotage, disappoint, or distract us from what God wants to do in the world or my life in Jesus's name. I bind you from holding me in bondage and trying to lock me up in death in Jesus's name. You will not steal my destiny. Lord, don't let Satan hinder my testimony. I bind and remove every obstacle in my way in Jesus's name. I plead the blood of Jesus over my spirit, soul, body, and life.

Thank You, Lord, that You have given me exceeding greatness of power as I believe in You. This power is far above all principalities, powers, might, dominions, and any other names that are named in this world. You have given me jurisdictional authority and power over all the power the enemy possesses, and these evil spirits will not hurt me in Jesus's name. I have physical and mental strength over and against the strategies and plots of every evil spirit.

I give glory to my living God that You have blotted out the transgressions that stood against me. My sins were contrary and hostile to me, but Jesus, You nailed them to Your cross. Because of Your love, I now know that You have disarmed every evil spirit that was ranged against me. Jesus, I laugh today because You made a public example of all devils and triumphed over them in what You did for us on the cross.

I thank You, Lord, that my body is wholly filled and flooded with God Himself. Therefore, I bind every evil spirit that would try to take over my life through mind control tactics and temptations enticing my flesh. Lord, I know that I am not wrestling against flesh and blood but against spiritual wickedness in high places, rulers of the darkness of this world, powers, and principalities. This is why I am thankful that You have given me Your power to bind their operation and render them powerless. I use that power today and declare that nothing shall by any means hurt me. Father, I have made Jesus my Lord, and because He rules me, nothing else can ever control or rule me again. Amen.

21

PRAYERS FOR ENERGY AND STRENGTH

Exodus 15:2 (NIV); Nehemiah 8:10; Psalm 28:7–8; Isaiah 40:31; 41:10; Joel 3:10; 2Corinthians 13:9; Ephesians 3:16; 6:10; Philippians 4:13; Hebrews 12:3 (MSG)

My Notes:

Always remember that the joy of the Lord is our strength. So never let the enemy or tests and trials steal your joy. If you want to keep your joy, you must learn to live in God's grace. When we are living in and by grace, we will never be in our own human ability. Also, we will see God do for us what we cannot do for ourselves. This is pure grace when we have none of our human efforts involved in trying to accomplish things in life. We have to fully trust God for all things. Now we see why the Word says in Philippians 4:13 that we can do all things through Christ who gives us strength. The Amplified Bible says that Jesus infuses us with inner strength.

When we are at our weakest, God gets to be the strongest. Second Corinthians 13:9 says, "For we are glad, when we are weak, and ye are strong: and this also we wish, even for your perfection" (KJV). We will not be perfected until we are in Christ's ability and everything He did for us on the cross. Check out Hebrews 12:3

in the Message Bible, which says, "When you find yourselves flagging in your faith, go over that story again, item, by item, that long litany of hostility he plowed through, That will shoot adrenaline into your souls!" This is saying when you find yourself weak in faith and doubting a bit, go over the story of Jesus line by line, which will shoot fresh new believing and strength in your brain. God promised to be with us and strengthen us in Isaiah 41. Because of this promise, He told us not to fear or be dismayed.

In fact, in Exodus 15:2 we find that, "The Lord is my strength and my defense, he has become my salvation. He is my God, and I will praise him, my father's God, and I will exalt him" (NIV). When you exalt the Lord, you make Him bigger than whatever you are facing. When you exalt and praise Him as your strength, He empowers you with all that He is. Keep speaking that we are "strong in the Lord and the power of His might" (Ephesians 6:10 KJV).

Prayer:

Thank You, Lord, that You are my strength and my song; only You can give me the victory. I'm looking to You for victory today. Also, Your Word says that Your joy, oh Lord, is my strength and that I can do all things through Christ who gives me strength. Lord Jesus, I thank You for infusing inner strength into me. Therefore, I rebuke fatigue and tiredness. I thank You, Lord, that my body is quickened and made alive by the power of the Holy Spirit. The same power that raised Jesus from the dead is raising my body up to a heavenly state of being and dignity. Because of your power I am alert, sharp, and active.

I praise You, Lord, that today, right now, my body is being energized, strengthened, quickened, renewed, and restored by the power of God. I speak restoration to my joints, cells, organs, and tissues in Jesus's name. Oh Lord, I praise You for Your endless energy and boundless, supernatural strength. I thank You for the angels who minister to my body as I sleep. They are supernaturally recharging and refreshing me right now.

I thank You, Lord, that I wait for You, and You renew my youth and strength like the eagles. I thank You, Lord, that I run and do not get weary and walk and do not faint. I am strong in You, Lord, and in the power of Your might. I praise You that You give power to the faint and to them that have no might, You increase their strength.

Glory to God that You continually grant me, according to the riches of Your glory, to be strengthened with might by Your spirit in my inner man. I praise You, Lord, that my spirit man, and therefore my body, are strong and alert. I am truly empowered through my union with You. Lord, I draw my strength from the strength that Your boundless might provides.

I also thank You for balance in life. You give me wisdom to know when to rest and when to work with diligence and urgency. I am equipped for every service and work that You have called me to by the power of the Holy Spirit. Lord, not only are You the strength of my life, but You are my shield. My heart trusts in You, and I am helped. Therefore, my heart continually rejoices, and with a song, I will forever praise You. Lord, You are the saving strength of my life because I am Your anointed one. Lord, instead of speaking that I am weak, I will declare that I am strong because of Your power working through me. Lord, I need Your power to flow through me and fill every dry place. Let Your grace or the ability of Your unconditional love for me do in me what I cannot do for myself. I am full of strength in Jesus's name. Amen.

22

PRAYERS FOR EXPECTANT MOTHERS

Genesis 3:16; 22:17; Exodus 23:25–26; Deuteronomy 28:4; Psalm 112:2; 113:9; 127:3; 139:13–16; Proverbs 18:21; Isaiah 44:3; 54:17; Matthew 18:17–20; John 10:10; 14:14; Romans 4:17; Galatians 3:13; 1 Timothy 2:13–15; 1 Peter 2:24

My Notes:

A curse was pronounced upon Adam and Eve when they ate the fruit from the tree of the knowledge of good and evil in Genesis 3:16. Specifically, death entered the world and "to the woman [God] said: "I will multiply your sorrow and conception; in pain you shall bring forth children; your desire shall be for your husband, and he shall rule over you." However, all of this happened before Jesus came on the scene and paid the price for all our sins. He died, taking the penalty that you and I deserved for what we had done wrong. Because of Jesus's sacrifice, we can now live free from every curse. Galatians 3:13 says, "Christ hath redeemed us from the curse of the law, being made a curse for us" (KJV). We discussed what the curse of the law was earlier in this book. Remember, part of the curse was sickness and disease.

Another verse to look at is 1 Timothy 2:13–15. "For Adam was formed first, then Eve. And Adam was not deceived, but the woman being deceived, fell into transgression.

Nevertheless she will be saved in childbearing if they continue in faith, love, and holiness with self-control." "She will be saved in childbearing" means because of the birth of Jesus, who was divine. Yes, curses came because of the deception of Eve. But, God also did something quite extraordinary by causing the world's salvation and answer to come through the womb of a woman. Jesus's birth means total defeat to all curses, including pain during labor. He purchased our freedom from everything that is not total victory, peace, and success, even stomach cramps.

For this reason, mothers, you must know that life and death are in the power of your tongue. You will eat the fruit of or have the things that you have been believing and speaking. Therefore, while you are pregnant or trying to get pregnant, you must not speak any negativity, doubt, or unbelief based on how circumstances look or how you feel. Speak Jesus's words of life over every situation or problem. His words contain the life of God, healing, prosperity, victory, success, peace, and miracle-working power.

Don't forget that we have angels or ministering spirits who watch over us and help bring Jesus's words to pass. They also protect us from any and all hurt, harm, or danger when we command them to. Angels are activated and go to work for us based on the words that we believe and speak by faith. Therefore, speak life, health, and success over you and your unborn fetus. The Word says to call those things that be not as though they were in Romans 4:17.

With this in mind, go ahead and claim the promises of God over your pregnancy, delivery, and child's life. Speak that you will carry your baby to full-term without complications or curses, including morning sickness. Know Galatians 3:13 like the back of your hand and keep speaking that you have been redeemed from the curse of breaking God's laws. This gives you complete freedom from all complications, discomforts, and distressing bodily ailments caused by and associated with pregnancy or childbirth.

Prayer:

Lord, You promised Abraham that in blessing, You would bless him, and in multiplying, You would multiply his descendants. You promised that his descendants would multiply as the stars in the heavens and as the sand on the seashore. I am a descendant of Abraham because of Jesus. Therefore, I thank You for allowing me to multiply mightily upon the earth. Thank You, Lord, for many children.

God, I am so thankful that you grant the barren woman a home and the right to be a joyful mother of children. Because I do what You say, I will not be barren or cast my young through miscarriages before their time. I will produce and not be barren because of Your power working in my womb. I bind every evil spirit that would try to kill, steal, or destroy my baby's life in Jesus's name. No weapon formed against my fetus shall prosper. I plead the blood of Jesus over my spirit, soul, body, and baby in Jesus's name. Jesus, You said that You came that we might have life and have it more abundantly. Therefore, I will not fear death for me or my unborn child. When my child comes forth, I will have exceeding joy and delight in them. For children are a heritage from You.

Thank You, Lord, that I serve You and You bless my bread and water and You take morning sickness from my midst. Lord, I thank You that Jesus set me free from morning sickness when He died on the cross. He also took stripes on His back so I could be healed and made whole. Morning sickness is a part of the curse of breaking God's laws. You said that You have redeemed me from the curse of the law. Therefore, body, line up with the Word of God in Jesus's name. I can and I will be pregnant without morning sickness. I decree and declare that my pregnancy will be joyous and full of power. I bind any and all fatigue and tiredness in Jesus's name.

Lord, You cover my child/children in the womb. So I praise You, oh God, because my seed is fearfully and wonderfully made by You. Their frame was not hidden from You when they were made in secret. Your eyes saw their substance before they were formed, and You wrote and fashioned their days before the beginning of time. I praise You, Lord, for pouring out Your spirit on my seed and blessings on my offspring. Thank You for anointing my baby from the womb. Fill my baby with the Holy Spirit and fire from the womb. My baby will serve the Lord with joy and gladness all the days of their life.

Lord, Your Word says, "Whatever I ask in your name, you will do it." Therefore, I ask that every system forming in my child will work in the proper order as it is designed to function in heaven. Thank You, Lord, that my baby will form in perfect peace and divine health. I believe the respiratory, nervous, circulatory, and digestive systems will be complete and whole with no defects. Thank You that the angels above are helping my baby's cardiovascular, digestive, endocrine, immune, integumentary, lymphatic, muscular, nervous, reproductive, respiratory, skeletal, and urinary systems form by the power of God. Angels are already assigned to protect me and my baby from any and all danger and harm. My baby's brain will function at the highest capacity possible because my bundle of blessings will have the mind of Christ. My baby will be a trillion times smarter than the devil's children. Thank You, Lord, that the fruit of my womb is blessed. I praise You for perfectly knitting my child together in my womb.

The diseases of this earth and generation will not prosper in my child's body. No weapon formed against my fetus will prosper. I will not experience swelling of the feet, pregnancy-induced diabetes, or preeclampsia in Jesus's name. My child will not have any physical or mental illness of any kind. I am totally healthy and so is my baby.

Lord, I ask and thank You for a quick, fast, and speedy pain-free delivery in Jesus's name. I declare that my delivery will be stress-free and complication-free. I command my uterus and pelvis to open up without pain at the right time in Jesus's name. Thank You, Lord, that I will not suffer any tearing or injuries of any kind. I will not go into labor early, but I will carry my baby full-term. Once my baby is born, he or she will nurse without complications.

Thank You, Lord, for total peace during and after my labor. I and my baby will both be perfectly whole. Thank You, Jesus, for giving my doctors or midwife wisdom and knowledge to make the right decisions concerning my care and that of my baby. Father, I will experience Your anointing and the power of Your presence during the whole labor process.

Father, thank You that my seed shall be mighty upon the earth. My children are a part of the generation of the upright. Therefore, they are blessed. They will preach the gospel, lay hands on the sick, and be continually filled with the Spirit. Amen.

23

PRAYERS FOR THE LOST (NEED SALVATION)

Psalm 2:8; Isaiah 54:17; Matthew 9:38; 18:3; Luke 10:1–2, 17; John 10:4–5; Ephesians 1:18; 3:19; Philippians 2:5; 2 Timothy 2:26

My Notes:

Psalm 2:8 says, "Ask of Me, and I will give You the nations as Your inheritance, and the uttermost parts of the earth as Your possession" (AMP). Therefore, in prayer, we should be asking the Lord for souls daily. This is our inheritance from the Father. Soul winners are the happiest people on earth. Jesus sent the disciples out two by two ahead of Him to the places He was about to visit in Luke 10:1. Verse 17 said that the seventy people that He sent out returned with joy. They learned that as they were obeying the Lord, the devils were subject to them through Jesus's name.

Jesus taught in Matthew 9:38 that we should "pray therefore to the Lord of the harvest, that he will send forth laborers into his harvest." The Darby Bible Translation says that we should supplicate for people who do not know Jesus as their Lord and Savior. This means we should really be praying or interceding on behalf of those who need to be saved. In Romans 5:10, "saved" means to be daily delivered from sin's dominion, power, or control (AMPC).

145

The dictionary says that supplication is the action of asking or begging for something earnestly or humbly.[41] Therefore, we need to seek the Lord diligently on behalf of those who are lost. The Geneva Study Bible says that we should literally pray for the Lord to cast the laborers out to preach the gospel. They should be cast out because men are very slow in a work that is so holy. Our prayer should be for God to send a person to teach or preach the gospel to people in a way they can understand so that they may give their whole heart to Him. Let's pray for those who are in need of salvation right now.

Prayer:

Thank You, Lord, for bringing _____ (fill in the name) to the knowledge of the truth that is in Christ Jesus. Have mercy on _____ (fill in the name). Give her/him a personal revelation of Your love and power. May the eyes of her/his understanding be enlightened that she/he may know the hope to which You have called them on this earth. Show her/him who You made her/him in Christ Jesus.

I bind Satan off her/his mind in Jesus's name. Thank You, Lord, for giving them the mind of Christ. Let that same mind, which was in Christ Jesus, be also in _____ (fill in the name).

Lord, I pray that You send laborers to preach the gospel to _____ (fill in the name) in a way that he/she can understand that he/she may give his/her whole life to You. Let _____ (fill in the name) hear Your voice, and the voice of a

---

41   *Merriam-Webster*, s.v., "supplication (*n.*)," accessed March 4, 2020, https://www.merriam-webster.com/dictionary/supplication.

stranger, he/she will not follow. Father, You said if we ask of You, You would give us the nations as our inheritance.

Therefore, I thank You that no weapon formed against _____ (fill in the name) shall prosper. I thank You that the knowledge of the truth that is in Christ Jesus will shine unto the life, mind, and heart of _____ (fill in the name). Let_____ (fill in the name) awake to Your righteousness and Your standards in life. I thank You for sending the right laborers across his/her path that can preach the gospel to_____ (fill in name) in a way that he/she can understand. I pray that _____ (fill in name) will give You every area of his/her life and not hold back one area from You. Thank You, Father, that You're setting _____ (fill in name) free from anger, frustration, and all of the hindrances of their past. You're that type of God: a miracle-working God and a Creator who loves us.

Thank You, Lord, that _____ (fill in the name) comes back to their right senses and that they can escape from the snare of the devil. I thank You, Lord, that he/she will no longer be held captive by the enemy and that You will free them for Your will. Let them be truly converted and turn toward God in holiness in every area of their lives in Jesus's name. Amen.

24

PRAYERS FOR SALVATION

John 3:16; 10:10, 17–19; Romans 6:23; 8:3, 37; 10:9, 13; 2 Corinthians 5:17

My Notes:

Remember, as I said earlier, "saved" means to be daily delivered from sin's dominion, power, or control, according to Romans 5:10. To be saved, a person must make a confession of faith with their mouth and believe something in their heart. You confess with your mouth the Lord Jesus and then believe in your heart what Jesus did for us on the cross. God sent Jesus to the earth to show us His love for humanity. Man messed up by living in sin. Because of sin, man was stripped of God's glory and honor. Now, God needed a way to get His presence back to man. God needed a perfect sacrifice without spot or blemish to take the punishment for sin so that man did not and does not have to take it. For the wage or paycheck for sin is some form of death or whatever God is not. God represents life, health, prosperity, peace, joy, and more. Everything that is evil or bad is a form of death that comes from the evil one or whatever God is not.

Jesus became our substitute and perfect sacrifice. He came in the guise of sinful flesh and as an offering for sin to defeat sin in the flesh. Now sin no longer has control over us to make us obey its lust and power. Jesus had never done anything wrong, but God laid all our sins on Him, and He died a physical death. However, God did not leave Jesus in what was wrong with us.

Instead, God raised Jesus from death to life and from all our sins on the third day. That is the power for us to escape any dead or hopeless situation we might face in life. God could legally raise Jesus from the dead because death had illegally wrapped itself around Him. Death only has power where there is sin. When there is no sin, the enemy cannot find a place in us. Jesus never committed a sin; He only took our place who sinned. Therefore, sin could not legally keep Jesus locked up in death. This means the Father could legally raise Jesus up and out of everything that was wrong with the whole world. "God condemned sin in the flesh [subdued, overcame, and deprived it of its power over all who accept Jesus' sacrifice]" (AMPC). This is why Paul wrote and declared in the Bible, "O death, where is thy victory? O death, where is thy sting?" Glory to God who has resurrection power for us.

It is powerful to note that no one took Jesus's life. He willingly laid it down for us so that we could have His quality of life on earth as it is in heaven. Jesus said in John 10:10, "the thief comes only in order to steal and kill and destroy. I came that they may have and enjoy life, and have it in abundance (to the full, till it overflows)"(AMPC). Jesus then stated later in John 10:17–19, "Therefore doth my Father love me, because I lay down my life, that I might take it again. No man taketh it from me, but I lay it down of myself. I have power to lay it down, and I have power to take it again. This commandment have I received of my Father."

Prayer:

Lord, I believe You sent Jesus to die on the cross for me to show me Your love and to take my sins away. I believe that You died a physical death because all my sins were laid on You. But I believe that God's mighty power raised You, Jesus, from death to life on the third day. That is the power for me to be free from any dead or hopeless situation that I may face in life. Come into my heart, Lord Jesus, and save me. I turn from darkness to light and from the power of Satan unto God for Jesus to be my new Lord and new Master. I thank You, Lord Jesus, for saving me so that I will never be the same in Jesus's name.

Lord, Your Word says that whosoever shall call upon the name of the Lord shall be saved. I'm calling on You, and I believe You are saving me right now. Dear God, Your Word says that You so loved this world that You gave us Your only begotten Son. You said that whosoever believes in, trusts in, clings to, or relies on Jesus should not perish, come to destruction, or be lost. Instead, we could have eternal or everlasting life. Father, I am a whosoever who believes in Jesus, and I thank You right now for giving me everlasting life. I want to spend all of eternity with You forever. Amen.

You are now a new creature in Christ Jesus, and the old parts of you are now passed away. Behold, all things have become new for you. Now let's forget the past and look forward to the future! We have an expectation that something good will now happen to us. We no longer have any expectations of danger. Never forget that you are the best because the best lives in You, but only if Christ is there.

Let us rejoice and triumph that we have the victory and authority over all the works of darkness through Jesus Christ our Lord. Romans 8:37 says, "No, despite all these things, overwhelming victory is ours through Christ, who loved us" (NLT). Therefore, no matter what we go through in life, as long as we take Jesus and His teachings to God in prayer, we will win every battle and gain a surpassing victory.

After we triumph and win the battle, we can throw a party and celebrate our victory. Hallelujah! God's light explodes and breaks out and breaks through all the darkness.

Let us scream, "Hallelujah!" knowing we have triumphed in Jesus's name. Amen.

Made in the USA
Columbia, SC
29 August 2020

17105835R00098